THE COMPLETE GUIDE TO AUSSIEDOODLES

Vanessa Richie

Publication Data

Vanessa Richie

The Complete Guide to Aussiedoodles---- First edition.

Summary: "Successfully raising a Aussiedoodle Dog from puppy to old age" --- Provided by publisher.

ISBN: 978-1-71033-0-816

[1.Aussiedoodle Dogs --- Non-Fiction] I. Title.

Design by Sorin Rădulescu

First paperback edition, 2019

Cover Photo Courtesy of Joyce Wallace - Pecan Place Poodles and Poos

TABLE OF CONTENTS

INTRODUCTION

A designer dog, the Aussiedoodle is not quite as well known as the Labradoodle or Goldendoodle, but like these breeds, Aussiedoodles are incredibly popular – and for very good reason. Their intelligence is often compared to that of children, which means that not only does the breed have a wealth of energy, but they also have the ability to learn a lot. Both the Australian Shepherd and the Poodle are working dogs, which makes for a fantastic, hardworking mix.

The Aussiedoodle has a wide variety of looks. Some dogs on the small side of the medium-sized spectrum come in at about 25 pounds, but they can grow to be as much as 75 pounds. When you adopt an Aussiedoodle puppy, you have to be prepared for this huge disparity in size – and that's why it is so important to get information about the parents when you talk to breeders. You will want a rough idea of how big the puppy will be as an adult, which means asking about the Poodle side of the family.

Both parent breeds are notoriously loving dogs. The Aussiedoodle will want to be with you all the time, no matter where you go, and separation anxiety is something that you may have to monitor for in puppies and rescued adults. Be prepared for a dog that sticks to you like Velcro and loves to cuddle with your family.

Like their appearance, the problems you may encounter with your Aussiedoodle are unpredictable, although learning more about the parents can help you to decrease the likelihood that your pup will suffer from the typical genetic ailments of both parent breeds. Though Aussiedoodles are a fairly new breed, they have been around long enough to have an estimated life span of 12 years. It won't seem like nearly long enough with your sweet, cuddly little mischief maker!

CHAPTER 1
Breed History And Characteristics

Aussiedoodles, also known as Aussie-Poos, are a designer breed established a few years after the Labradoodle. They're a cross between a Poodle and an Australian Shepherd. Usually the mother is an Australian Shepherd because the puppies may be difficult for a purebred Poodle to carry without complications. The breed is too new to be recognized by any of the major dog organizations, such as the American Kennel Club. This means there is no standard for their appearance or temperament. Over time this may change, but for now, adopting an Aussiedoodle means you are getting a bit of a wildcard in terms of size and looks, though their temperament is fairly predictable.

Though Aussiedoodles may have a very short history, both of their parent breeds have been around for a long time. To understand what you are getting into with an Aussiedoodle, you have to understand the history of the Australian Shepherd and the Poodle. And the history of both breeds has one thing in common – they have been bred to be working dogs.

Photo Courtesy of
Ashley Schow
Cottonwood Creek Doodles

Australian Shepherds

The Australian Shepherd has a bit of a mysterious origin and has been called by several other names, including Bob-Tail, California Shepherd, New Mexican Shepherd, Pastor Dog, and Spanish Shepherd. It is believed that the dogs originated in Spain, then made their way around the world during the Age of Discovery as the Spanish travelled around the world. The dogs likely ended up in Australia and then made their way to the US. Despite the name, it seems that the breed as it is today was primarily bred in the US, particularly along the West Coast, where the breed probably arrived from Australia.

The dogs became incredibly popular in Colorado, where sheep-herding dogs were required during the 19th and 20th centuries. Despite probably being brought to the US from Australia, the breed's name could have come from the kind of sheep that they herded.

The Australian Shepherd dates back to the Victorian Era. They were bred from a number of different European breeds to help with shepherding sheep and cattle, and this definitely reflects in their personality and intellect. The adults are considered medium sized and are slightly longer than they are tall. They can be stubborn if they aren't trained early, a very common problem with many intelligent dogs. But they are loyal and loving, which is why they are popular – the American Kennel Club ranks them in the top 20 most popular breeds.

Poodles

The Poodle originated in Germany, descended from an Asian canine breed, and is one of the oldest pure breeds in existence. Some experts believe that they arrived with the Goths from western Asia and that they were used as hunting companions. The unique curls to their coats give away their ties to the Asian breeds, and they are likely related to many of the European water dogs that also have curly fur.

From the beginning, Poodles were working dogs. The German tribes used them as hunting dogs, and there are people in Europe who still have this breed accompany them on hunting trips. In France, they became popular companions for duck hunters because of the way their fur seemed to repel water. Over time, Poodles became working dogs in many other professions, such as the military, although their temperament did not make them nearly as effective as some of the other popular guard dogs today. Where they really thrived was as circus performers and entertainers.

Just like the Australian Shepherd, Poodles are intelligent and loving. They also don't tend to be stubborn (though they do require early training like any other intelligent breed), which is why they have been so popular as entertainers. They have a largely easygoing personality and enjoy engaging with their owners in fun tricks and games. There is a very good reason why this breed has been so incredibly popular for so long – it is incredibly versatile. While no dog is fully hypoallergenic, most people can live with Poodles without suffering from allergies. All of this coupled with how affectionate they can be, and Poodles are a fantastic choice for virtually any home.

With the Poodle parent having such a long and close history with humans, the Aussiedoodle is almost certain to be easily integrated into your family. Even if your pup gets some of the stubbornness of the Australian Shepherd, your newest family member is going to have a lot of great qualities from both sides.

A Brief History Of The Aussiedoodle

There isn't much known about the history of the Aussiedoodle. The breed is still relatively new to the dog community, but it is thought that the Aussiedoodle came into play sometime within the last twenty years. This is due to the rising popularity of the Labradoodle and Bernedoodle, which have a more notable history. Like other designer dogs, it is presumed that the Aussiedoodle was first born in the United States.

Today the Aussiedoodle has no notable ancestors, and it is not eligible for registration, so it cannot be recognized as a pedigree even if both parents are purebred.

One of the main reasons the Aussiedoodle has skyrocketed into popularity is due to their hypoallergenic properties and the boom of "Doodle" breeds. Besides that, the dog is a combination of two dogs that have been around for centuries and are known for their characteristics such as intelligence, loyalty, and all-around good nature.

The Aussiedoodle does come in three different types as well. There is your standard Aussiedoodle that is the cross between a standard Australian Shepherd and a Standard Poodle. The Mini or Miniature Aussiedoodle is a cross between an Australian Shepherd and a Miniature Poodle. The Miniature Aussiedoodle tends to weight around 20 to 40 pounds. Then the Toy Aussiedoodle is a combination of an Australian Shepherd and a Toy Poodle. The Toy Aussiedoodle typically sits below 20 pounds.

Photo Courtesy of
Soleil Carroll

Although the history of the Aussiedoodle is brief, this dog breed is becoming increasingly popular as the years go on. In a few years more information and history will be available about the Aussiedoodle.

Photo Courtesy of Ashley LeMaster

Knowing The Variations

"Each puppy will inherit the different traits of the parent breeds to a different degree. There is no breed standard, but there is a wonderful variety of combinations, truly something for everyone."

Adrian Booher
Sunset Hill Farm

When it comes to an Aussiedoodle, there are a few crossbreeds that can affect the decision on what type of Aussiedoodle you want. This is known as F1 Aussiedoodle, F1B Aussiedoodle, and F2B Aussiedoodle. The main differences between these Aussiedoodles are their coats and the type of dog they were bred with.

The F1 Aussiedoodle is a mixture of an Australian Shepherd and a Standard Poodle. The coat on this dog is usually straight, but it can be slightly wavy. This type of Aussiedoodle has a coat that is a mixture between the Australian Shepherd and the Poodle so that it can be somewhat longer but still has a little wave to it like a Poodle.

The F1B Aussiedoodle is a combination of an F1 Aussiedoodle and a Standard Poodle. The F1B Aussiedoodle has a wavy to curly coat, more like a Poodle, and out of the two are the least likely to shed. If you have mild pet allergies, the F1B Aussiedoodle might be more up your alley.

The F2B Aussiedoodle is a breed between an F1 Aussiedoodle and an F1B Aussiedoodle. This breed of Aussiedoodle will be fluffy and will require a little more work on their coat. The coat is easy to maintain but will require brushing when it grows out. The coat will be similar to an Australian Shepherd with a little less fluff.

Now you might be wondering what the big deal is between an F1 and an F1B Aussiedoodle. Since these dogs

FUN FACT
Hypoallergenic?

Many Aussiedoodle breeders claim that their puppies are hypoallergenic. However, people with allergies react to a dog's saliva and dander, so no dog is truly hypoallergenic. Having said that, some people with allergies seem to have reduced reactions to certain dog breeds, including Poodles. If you have allergies, an Aussiedoodle that is three-fourths Poodle may not trigger your allergies.

Photo Courtesy of
Kristin-Annie Espinoza

aren't purebred and aren't recognized by the American Kennel Club, the F1 or F1B is a big deal to some owners, since they have purebred parents. An F1 breed of Aussiedoodle is the result of a purebred Australian Shepherd that was bred with a purebred Poodle. The F1B is taking a dog that is 50%-50% Australian Shepherd/Poodle cross and breeding it back to a parent breed. By parent breed, we mean either an Australian Shepherd or a Poodle.

Photo Courtesy of Natasha Gussack

FUN FACT
Other Names

While Aussiedoodle is the most common name for this breed, other names include Aussiepoo, Aussie Poodle, and Australian Shepherd Poodle Mix/Cross.

An F2 Aussiedoodle is a dog that was bred with the first generation of Aussiedoodles. So, it could be two F1s bred together or an F1, and an F1B bred together. If you hear about an F3, which isn't often when talking about an Aussiedoodle, then it is a litter that is a mixture of an F1B to F1B or an F2 to an F2 or any combination of higher generation Aussiedoodles.

CHAPTER 2
Loyal, Loving Ball Of Energy With A Constant Need To Be With You

"The very best trait of this breed is versatility. If you breed some breeds, i.e. German Shepherds, you could rule out 95% of the buyers as not suitable homes for the breed. However, with an Aussiedoodle, most buyers are suitable due to this breeds ability to adapt to almost any situation. This is what makes them so highly suitable for service/therapy work also."

Joyce Wallace
Pecan Place Aussiedoodles

The growing popularity of Aussiedoodles is entirely understandable. They aren't as big as many other dogs with similar intellects and temperaments. They are a real pleasure to have around, and they can keep up with you during your most rigorous workouts. Aussiedoodles quickly become an integral part of their human family. Be aware that they can be a bit stubborn, so you'll need to be firm with your new companion right from the beginning.

*Photo Courtesy of
Jordyn Neal*

*Photo Courtesy of
Jolyne Lavoie*

Descriptions And Defining Characteristics

"The best thing about a litter is that each of the puppies is a unique blend of the Poodle coat and poise and the energy and friendship of the Aussie. Some lean more toward energy and some lean more toward calm. Both breeds share high intelligence and an intuitive connection with their people, which makes every puppy awesome."

Adrian Booher
Sunset Hill Farm

One of the attractions of this particular breed is that you have no idea exactly what your dog will look like as an adult. Spend a couple of minutes checking out images of this breed, and you will see that no two Aussiedoodles look alike, to the point that it can be difficult to tell that they are the same breed. If you decide to adopt a puppy, you will find that even in the same litter, the puppies are all incredibly unique.

What pretty much remains the same is that wonderful temperament. Since the temperament of both parent breeds is fairly similar, an Aussiedoodle typically is a fantastic loving little ball of energy that will want to be with you wherever you go.

Photo Courtesy of
Carolina Cantieri

Appearance

"The number one unexpected thing a Aussiedoodle owner may encounter is the color change of the coat. Some Aussiedoodles carry a gene that changes the color of the coat within the first year. I always tell potential Aussiedoodle owners that as far as the color of the coat goes, buying an Aussiedoodle is like playing the lottery: you don't know what you'll end up with. I have seen puppies go home chocolate or even merle and on their first birthday they are cream in color. Then there are others that stay the same color they went home as. It just all depends if they are a carrier of the 'Color Changing Gene'."

Brey Sanchez
Marley's Doodles

Without any defining features, your Aussiedoodle's appearance will be completely unique – there will be no mistaking your dog for anyone else's at the dog park. Depending on the size of the Poodle parent, your Aussiedoodle can range in size between 25 and 75 pounds. The Aussiedoodle is considered a medium-sized dog, but those that are on the larger side of the spectrum can fall into the large-dog category. If you want to get an idea of your puppy's adult size, look at the Poodle papa.

The breed's coat colors are entirely unpredictable. Some Aussiedoodles have the bluish look associated with Australian Shepherds, but with the curliness of the Poodle coat. Others can be a Poodle color (black, white, apricot/cream, blue, or silver) with the longer hair of the Shepherd.

One eye-catching aspect of the Aussiedoodle is their potential eye color. You will find many with the cold blue of the Australian Shepherd, but just as many with the soft eyes of a Poodle. It is also possible that your Aussiedoodle will have heterochromia iridium or heterochromia iridis – either their eyes will be two different colors or they will have several colors in their eyes.

HELPFUL TIP
Exercise is Crucial

Most Aussiedoodles will not be content as couch potatoes. Both Australian Shepherds and Poodle were bred to work all day, so Aussiedoodles usually have lots of energy. Plan on walking your Aussiepoo at least an hour and a half every day. A run around the dog park or an agility course is even better.

Photo Courtesy of Shelby Robinson

There is no standard or norm for any other aspect of the breed either. They may have the svelte look of the Poodle, or the more robust and sturdy body of the Australian Shepherd. Odds are you will need to keep them trimmed to really see their bodies as their hair does tend to be longer than a Poodle's but with a similar texture.

Temperament

As varied as their look is, their temperament is fairly uniform, and you will find that there are four adjectives already closely associated with the Aussiedoodle – devoted, playful, loving, and energetic. Another word often used to describe them is intelligent, though they can hide that behind their adorable little faces. They absolutely love to play, and will bring you a toy just to pull it away from you at the last second. Being teased by your dog will probably devolve into a playing session, even if you were in the middle of doing chores or homework. Turning down those hopeful eyes that just want to play with you will be incredibly difficult, and is why you will need a regular schedule for working out your puppy's energy.

Once an Aussiedoodle becomes a part of your family, the dog will pretty much glue itself to the side of anyone who is at home. Training is a great way to help get rid of excess energy, as well as spending some quality time bonding. However, you may spend a good bit of time working through a bit of the Australian Shepherd's stubbornness before you can fully enjoy the training sessions. Once they understand how training works, the sky is pretty much the limit. When you have visitors, your dog will love to show off what she knows and will lap up the attention.

Aussiedoodles can be great companions to children as well. They can join in yard adventures and keep your children occupied on days when they can't play outside and you don't want them playing video games or watching TV all day. It is best not to leave Aussiedoodles alone with small children – the eagerness of a young child coupled with any high energy dog is a bad mix. To ensure that your dog doesn't accidentally hurt your young child, you must always closely monitor their interaction to keep either of them from getting too overexcited.

Beyond stubbornness, another potential Australian Shepherd trait that you will want to watch for in your Aussiedoodle is a desire to herd. It can be incredibly cute when your dog is young, especially when she starts rounding up your children, but it won't be cute for long. If your puppy exhibits herding behavior, socialization and training can help you minimize the issue before it becomes a problem.

Photo Courtesy of
Jenny Rcomnie

The Ideal Environment For An Aussiedoodle

So long as you are able to give your young friend lots of regular exercise, you can bring your Aussiedoodle into any kind of home, small or large. Although it is impossible to predict just how big your dog will be, she won't be extremely large, so you won't need a huge amount of space either inside or outside.

A Yard Isn't Necessary – But Regular Exercise Is

"The Aussiedoodle is an ACTIVE hybrid. Be sure that you have the time and energy for the interaction your pup will need before you purchase a puppy."

Sheron MW Steele, PhD
XANADU of the Rockies

It isn't absolutely necessary to have a yard when you have an Aussiedoodle, but if you don't you will need to plan for three to four long walks a day. You can do some inside training, but that won't be sufficient to tire out your puppy. Several daily walks are necessary, even if you do have a yard. Simply putting your dog outside and expecting your Aussiedoodle to tire herself out does not work, and will likely result in your yard being torn up. That is never the dog's fault – it's yours for putting a family dog outside when she is an indoor dog.

Taking your dog somewhere new to play will help keep her mentally and physically stimulated. This is advisable whether or not you have a yard. Hikes and jogs are also fantastic ways of making sure your Aussiedoodle gets adequate exercise.

A yard does make it easier to train and play with your canine. You can set up an obstacle course when your pup gets a bit older, and that will go a long way toward reducing how much and how far you have to walk.

Photo Courtesy of
Ashley Schow
Cottonwood Creek Doodles

Training And Socialization Required To Keep Your Aussiedoodle Toeing The Line

"They are real 'velcro dogs'! If you do not want your dog to follow you everywhere you go, an Aussiedoodle is not for you. They love their family! If trained from the start to play outside, and not inside the house, then you will have a calm quiet house dog that will lie either on your lap or at your feet (your choice)."

Pam Keith
Doodles Galore

Poodles are considered great, easy to train dogs. Australian Shepherds are fantastic dogs too, but they can have an independent streak that makes them more difficult to train. Training is absolutely essential because all intelligent dogs will look for ways to combat boredom, and that usually means tearing and shredding. To make sure your Aussiedoodle does not become a little demon in your home, you are going to need to start training her as early as possible. This may be a bit more work than if you just got a Poodle or a Retriever. But in the end, it's well worth the work.

Socialization will be easy because Aussiedoodles are predisposed to loving everyone and everything (though there may be a bit of an instinct to chase small animals). The only thing you will need to watch for is your dog getting a little too frisky or overenthusiastic, because she will be difficult to calm down. Training will help you make socialization a little less chaotic.

Not A Breed For Beginners

Poodles are on most organizations' lists for best breeds for first-time pet owners, including the American Kennel Club. However, Australian Shepherds generally are not recommended for people who have not had a dog before, especially if you have younger children. It is possible that your Aussiedoodle will take more after the calmness of the Poodle, but it may not. Spending time talking to the breeders can help you understand the dog. Ultimately though, working dogs that are known to herd are not good first dogs. Instead of taking a risk, it would probably be best to start with a Poodle or other recommended dog for a new pet parent. Once you have a bit of experience – especially with training – you can bring one of these amazing dogs into your home. There will be the added bonus of having an older, more mellow dog to help train your Aussiedoodle.

CHAPTER 3
Finding Your Aussiedoodle

If you are still reading, that probably means that you are sold on getting your own adorable Aussiedoodle to help you get in shape, play with your current dog, or just to be a companion that is always there for you. The breed's friendliness and intelligence make them a great addition to the family, so any excitement you are feeling is definitely justified.

The hunt to find your newest family member is going to take a while, even if you decide to rescue an adult. We strongly recommend avoiding pet stores to find your dog. Deciding to purchase a designer dog means that you are going to have a lot of research ahead of you, especially because you will have to be even more wary of puppy mills than with most other breeds. With fewer known issues, there are many problems that can result from improper breeding and care at the beginning of the Aussiedoodle's life. To ensure that you get a healthy puppy that will be your loving companion for as long as possible, you have to find a reputable breeder who cares more about the puppies than the money. With the Aussiedoodle's estimated 12-year life span, you want to have as much protection as possible against genetic ailments, and that means finding a breeder who makes sure their puppies are healthy.

Photo Courtesy of
Joyce Wallace
Pecan Place Poodles and Poos

Photo Courtesy of
La Toyia Forester

Unlike purebred dogs, the potential genetic problems for the Aussiedoodle cover two different breeds with fairly well documented health concerns. You should find out about the puppy's parents to ensure that your puppy has the best chance of living a healthy, happy life. It is also important to know what diseases are common to both of the parent breeds. This is typically not possible with adult dogs, but if you find a rescue, you may be able to get some of the dog's family history.

About Designer Dogs

While many designer dogs are bred for looks alone, the American Kennel Club pushes for pure breeds with longer histories and established temperaments, particularly those breeds that have declined in numbers, such as Otterhounds. The AKC's argument is that it is unnecessary for people to intentionally create a new breed because many older breeds have the same traits through normal selective breeding. It is easier to predict the potential risks and problems with a single breed than by trying to establish a consistent new breed through two different breeds.

The American Kennel Club's concerns are certainly legitimate, particularly because of puppy mills that seek to quickly profit from designer dog trends. As will be covered in a later chapter, looking into the parents' health and history is just as important for designer dogs as it is for purebred dogs. You want to find a breeder who knows the parents well and takes very good care of them. You also want to find a breeder who can tell you about the parents, their personalities, and their parentage so that you can have a rough idea of what the temperament and health of the puppy will be. For designer dogs, you want to find breeders who love dogs and know how to breed them right, and not people who are simply trying to make a lot of money off of the newest trend. The fact that you are getting a designer breed means that you have enough variables without adding the potential problems that are created by uncaring breeders.

Puppy Versus Adult

Deciding to adopt an Aussiedoodle is just the beginning. From there you need to decide whether you want to adopt a puppy or an adult. There are positive and negatives to both options, just like with every breed. The approach to adopting an Aussiedoodle is the same as it is for most other breeds. However, with a protective dog like the Aussiedoodle, you are going to want to ask a lot more questions about adopting an adult than with other breeds. Depending on the dog's age, you may need to consider the pros and cons of both adopting a puppy and rescuing an adult dog.

Adopting A Puppy

All puppies are a lot of work, starting with the moment the puppy enters your care. While the breed's temperament is largely predictable, how you train and socialize your puppy will affect nearly every aspect of the dog's adult life. From the very beginning, you have to establish yourself and your family as the ones in charge so that your Aussiedoodle understands the hierarchy from the moment he enters your home. This can be exhausting because the dogs have a lot of energy from an early age. Without proper training and socialization, you may have a dog that is too rambunctious and destructive.

The work to prepare your home for your puppy's arrival begins long before your puppy arrives though. Puppy proofing the home is as time consuming as child proofing your home. It is essential to puppy proof your home, but you still have to keep a constant eye on your puppy after the little guy arrives. If you do not have the time to puppy proof your home, then you should consider getting an adult dog (you should probably also consider a different breed because an Aussiedoodle of any age brought into the home is going to be a large time investment).

Aussiedoodle puppies are absolutely adorable, and they don't really understand their own limitations. It is up to you to provide the protection they need to be safe and unharmed. You can expect a unique experience raising your puppy because they have so much personality and are very curious about the world around them.

On the plus side, you will have more time to live together with a puppy than with an adult. You will have records about the puppy and the puppy's parents, making it easier to identify the potential problems your Aussiedoodle may suffer. This makes it considerably easier to ensure your puppy stays healthy and to catch potential issues earlier.

Some people find it easier to bond with puppies than with adult dogs. A young puppy is going to be nervous in a new home, but most adjust quickly because they are predisposed to enjoying the company of those around them. Your primary job will be protecting your puppy and making sure that you patiently train him. We will cover this more in a later chapter.

HELPFUL TIP
What Size?

Aussiedoodles vary greatly in size depending on whether their Poodle parent was a Standard, Miniature, or Toy Poodle. As a result, Aussiedoodles can weigh anywhere from 25 to 70 pounds. You should know whether you're looking for a Standard, Miniature, or Toy Aussiedoodle before starting the search for your new family member.

Photo Courtesy of
Dan Oltersdorf

Rescuing An Adult Aussiedoodle

"There are many pups and dogs that need a new home; many are in shelters. Study that new dog and spend as much time at the rescue facility with the pup/dog as possible."

Sheron MW Steele, PhD
XANADU of the Rockies

Rescuing any dog comes with some inherent risks. While it is possible to find Aussiedoodle puppies at dog rescues, it is much more likely that you will find a rescued adult.

Adopting an older Aussiedoodle will require a lot of work, but it should not be challenging if you already have pets at home since they are such a gregarious breed. Aussiedoodle-specific rescue organizations are cautious about adopting out a rescue with personality and socialization issues (there are some, including dogs from puppy mills and those that had negligent or abusive owners before being rescued). Rescue shelters will be less careful, though they will definitely try to impress upon potential adopters the risks and problems they are likely to face with a specific Aussiedoodle. Usually, rescuing an adult Aussiedoodle is more of a risk with the dog's health than temperament though, since they are, as discussed earlier, designer dogs.

The benefits of rescuing an Aussiedoodle are very similar to adopting any rescue dog. Many of them aren't bad dogs, they just have some bad habits. The odds are very good that you aren't going to be starting from scratch with housetraining – which can be a huge plus for people who don't have time to train a stubborn puppy. Adult dogs are awake more often than puppies, and while it may take them a bit longer to warm up to you, you can bond much faster with an adult, depending on their age. Adult Aussiedoodles may be a bit more wary, especially if they feel abandoned or were previous-

CAUTION
Watch Out for Puppy Mills and Bad Breeders

Thanks to their recent popularity, Aussiedoodles are popular dogs for puppy mills and backyard breeders. These breeders don't care about the health of their puppies, and the breeding dogs may be kept in horrific conditions. Make sure you find a breeder who does health testing on his or her breeding dogs and raises the puppies in the home.

ly treated poorly, but that loving disposition will probably come out fairly quickly once they start to feel safe and at home. Your new dog may not to want to cuddle with you in the early days either, which may be a bit dispiriting, but give the dog time. Once your adult dog bonds with you, it will be like flipping an affection switch, and then you really could not ask for a more loving canine.

One thing that is similar to preparing your home for puppies is that you will want to dog proof your home for a rescue. You will need to have everything set up before the dog arrives. Most people think it isn't necessary to

Photo Courtesy of
Gabriel Chapman

prepare for an adult dog and fail to properly prepare. It will just be less time consuming than preparing a home for a puppy. You should not keep the Aussiedoodle adult locked up in a crate the majority of the time, so at least in the beginning you will need a large space for the dog to get familiar with you and your home as you assess the personality and capabilities of the rescued adult. It is a fairly important consideration, particularly if you have other dogs, as you will want to ensure harmony in the home.

You may not be able to get a complete health record for an adult Aussiedoodle, but it is more likely that you will find a dog that has already been spayed or neutered, as well as chipped. Unless you adopt an Aussiedoodle that has health issues (these should be disclosed by the rescue organization if available), rescues tend to be less costly at the first vet visit than puppies.

Older dogs give you more immediate gratification. You don't have to go through those sleepless nights with a new puppy or the endless frustration that comes with early types of training. Older Aussiedoodles let you get right into enjoying your dog as you go out on adventures, even if there is a period of mistrust and uncertainty. All intelligent, high energy dogs require a lot of time and attention as puppies. Bypassing that is a major part of the appeal of older dogs.

Finally, one of the biggest benefits of getting an adult (besides getting to skip housetraining) – they are already their full size. You don't have to guess or estimate the size your dog will be, making it far easier to get the right gear and dog supplies in the beginning.

Aussiedoodle Clubs And Rescues

There are a number of Poodle mix rescues in North America. With Poodles being mixed with a wide range of other popular breeds, coupled with the fact that they are not recognized by larger, established dog organizations, the community of Poodle mixes has created specific organizations to protect the new breeds:

- Poo Mix Rescue – Poodle mixes are incredibly common and popular, so this site has more than just Aussiedoodles, but it is well worth a look to see the dogs that need a home.
- Sugar Pine Doodles Australian Labradoodles
- New Spirit 4 Aussie Rescue, Inc. – A rescue that takes in Australian Shepherds and mixes.
- Doodle Rescue Collective

Adopting From A Breeder

"Temperament should be one of your top concerns, right there with health. If you're picking a puppy for children this is your priority. Lots of dogs are beautiful but may not have the right temperament. "

Donna Molitor
DoncieDoodles

Finding a responsible breeder is the best thing you can do for your puppy since good breeders work with only healthy parents, reducing the odds that a puppy will have serious health issues. There aren't too many certified breeders because of how new the breed is. Coupled with the booming popularity, puppy mills and less capable breeders are looking to make money quickly from that popularity. It is the reason you need to be particularly careful and plan to spend a lot of time researching before deciding on where to get your puppy.

Photo Courtesy of Sharon Goodyear

Health Tests and Certifications

"If they are promising 'no shed' you will want to check the curl in the coat but remember the puppy coat is much fuzzier than the adult coat. The real curl comes in later but you can check the ear rims for curl and even if the coat is only wavy, the ear rims will be curly which generally means the adult coat will have curl to it. The more curl to the coat the less they shed."

Pam Keith
Doodles Galore

A healthy puppy requires healthy parents and a clean genetic history. A good breeder keeps extensive records of each puppy and the parents. You will want to review each of the parents' complete history to understand what traits your puppy is likely to inherit. Pay attention to learning abilities, temperament, clinginess, and any personality trait you consider important. You can either request documents be sent electronically to you or get them when you visit the breeder in person.

It could take a while to review the breeder's information about each parent, but it is always well worth the time you spend studying and planning. The more you know about the parents, the better prepared you will be for your puppy. The great breeders will have stories and details about the parents so that you can read about them at your leisure.

When looking for an Aussiedoodle to adopt, there are a number of health concerns that you should ask breeders or rescue groups about. Unlike purebred breeds and designer dogs with longer histories, the Aussiedoodle does not have any set of standards or organizations that offer standards or recommended tests. That means that breeders are left to handle testing and certifications for whatever they think is necessary.

While there aren't any specific tests or certifications, since both parent breeds are purebreds, you can make sure that certain tests have been conducted on them to reduce the chance of passing down genetic disorders of their respective breeds.

Check with the breeders to see if health tests and certifications of the parents have been completed:

- Australian Shepherds should tested for hip dysplasia, Colobomas, detached retinas, epilepsy, persistent and pupillary membrane. Many of these issues are associated with their eyes.

- Poodles should be tested for gastric dilatation volvulus (bloat), hypothyroidism, Von Willebrand disease, Legg-Calve-Perthes disease, luxating patellas, Sebaceous adenitis, and glaucoma.

Contracts and Guarantees

Even though Aussiedoodles are designer dogs and there is not a standard set of tests, good breeders will still offer guarantees on their puppies. While many people consider mixed breeds to be healthier than pure breeds, mixing breeds does not eliminate known health problems, and puppies could actually inherit the problems of two breeds instead of just one. Breeder contracts and guarantees are meant to protect the puppies as much as they are meant to protect you.

If a breeder has a contract that must be signed, make sure that you read through it completely and are willing to meet all of the requirements prior to signing it. The contracts tend to be fairly easy to understand and comply with, but you should be aware of all the facts before you agree to anything. Beyond putting down the money for the puppy, signing the contract says that you are serious about how you plan to take care of the puppy to the best of your abilities by meeting the minimum requirements set forth by the breeder. A contract may also say that the breeder will retain the puppy's original registration papers, although you can get a copy of the papers.

The guarantee states what health conditions the breeder promises for their puppies. This typically includes details of the dog's health and recommendations on the next steps of the puppy's care once it leaves the breeder's facility. Guarantees may also provide schedules to ensure that the health care started by the breeder is continued by the new puppy parent. In the event that a major health concern is found, the puppy will need to be returned to the breeder. The contract will also explain what is not guaranteed. The guarantee tends to be very long (sometimes longer than the contract), and you should read it thoroughly before you sign it.

Aussiedoodle contracts usually come with a requirement to have the dog spayed or neutered once it reaches maturity (typically six months). The contract may also contain naming requirements, health details, and a stipulation for what will happen if you can no longer take care of the animal (the dog usually goes back to the breeder). It could also include information on what will happen if you are negligent or abusive to your dog.

Finding a Breeder

Now that you know some of the basics of what to expect, it is time to start talking to breeders. The goal is to determine which breeders are willing to take the time to patiently and thoroughly answer all of your questions. They should have as much love for their Aussiedoodles as they want you to feel for your new puppy. And they should want to make sure that their puppies go to good homes.

If you find someone who posts regular pictures and information about the parents and the progress of the mother's pregnancy and vet visits, that is a very good sign. The best breeders will not only talk about their dogs and the plans for the parents in the future, they will stay in contact with you after you take the puppy home and answer any questions as they arise. These are the kinds of breeders who are likely to have waiting lists. The active interest in knowing about what happens to the puppies later shows that they care a great deal about each individual dog.

It is likely that for each breeder you call, the conversation will last about an hour. If a breeder does not have time to talk and isn't willing to talk with you later, you can cross them off your list. After you have talked with each possible breeder, compare answers.

The following are some questions to ask. Make sure you take careful notes while interviewing the breeders:

- Ask if you can visit in person. The answer should always be yes, and if it isn't, you don't need to ask any further. Thank the breeder and hang up. Even if the breeder is located in a different state, they should allow you to visit the facility.

- Ask about the required health tests and certifications they have for their puppies. These points are detailed further in the next section, so make sure to check off the available tests and certifications for each breeder. If they don't have all of the tests and certifications, you may want to remove the breeder from consideration.

- Make sure that the breeder always takes care of all of the initial health requirements in the first few weeks through the early months, particularly shots. Puppies require that certain procedures be done before they leave their mother to ensure they are healthy. Vaccinations and worming typically start around six weeks after the puppies are born, then need to be continued every three weeks. By the time your puppy is old enough to come home, he should be well into the procedures, or even completely through with the first phases of these important health care needs.

- Ask if the puppy is required to be spayed or neutered before reaching a certain age of maturity. Typically, these procedures are done in the puppies' best interest.

- Find out if the breeder is part of an Aussiedoodle organization or group.

- Ask about the first phases of your puppy's life, such as how the breeder plans to care for the puppy during those first few months. They should be able to provide a lot of detail, and they should do this without sounding as though they are irritated that you want to know. They will also let you know how much training you can expect to be done prior to the puppy's arrival in your home. It is possible that the breeder may start housetraining the puppy. Ask how quickly the puppy has picked up on the training. You want to be able to pick up from where the breeder left off once your Aussiedoodle reaches your home.

- See what kind of advice the breeder gives about raising your Aussiedoodle puppy. They should be more than happy to help guide you to doing what is best for your dog because they will want the puppies to live happy, healthy lives. You should also be able to rely on a breeder's recommendations, advice, and additional care after the puppy arrives at your home. Basically, you are getting customer support, as well as a great chance of a healthy dog.

- How many breeds do they manage a year? How many sets of parents do the breeders have? Puppies can take a lot of time and attention, and the mother should have some down time between pregnancies. Learn about the breeder's standard operations to find out if they are taking care of the parents and treating them like valuable family members and not strictly as a way to make money.

Selecting Your Puppy

"You need to make sure this dog is the right fit for you and your family. Just like people all dogs have their own personality even if they are the same breed or from the same litter. some can be on the more mellow/shy side where some may be more outgoing and have a little more energy. It's what is right for you and your family."

Brey Sanchez
Marley's Doodles

Selecting your puppy should be done in person. However, you can start checking out your puppy after birth if the breeder is willing to share videos and pictures. When you are finally allowed to see the puppies in person, there are several things you need to check the puppies for before making your final decision. Some of the things that you are looking at are universal, regardless of breed, and other things are Aussiedoodle specific.

- Assess the group of puppies as a whole. If most or all of the puppies are aggressive or fearful, this is an indication of a problem with the litter or (more likely) the breeder. Here are a few red flags if displayed by a majority of the puppies
  - Tucked tails
  - Shrinking away from people
  - Whimpering when people get close
  - Constant attacking of your hands or feet (beyond pouncing)
- Notice how well each puppy plays with the others. This is a great indicator of just how well your puppy will react to any pets you already have.
- Notice which puppies greet you first, and which ones hang back to observe.
- The puppies should not be fat or underweight, which admittedly, can be difficult to tell with their coats. A swollen stomach is generally a sign of worms or other health problems.
- Puppies should have straight, sturdy legs. Splayed legs can be a sign that there is something wrong.
- Examine the puppy's ears for mites, which will cause discharge. The inside of the ear should be pink, not red or inflamed.
- The eyes should be clear and bright.
- Check the puppy's mouth for pink, healthy looking gums.
- Pet the puppy to check his coat for the following.
  - Ensure that the coat feels thick and full. If the breeders have allowed the fur to get matted or really dirty, it is an indication that they likely are not taking proper care of the animals.
  - Check for fleas and mites by running your hand from the head to the tail, then under the tail (fleas are more likely to hide under most dogs' tails). Mites may look like dandruff.
- Check the puppy's rump for redness and sores, and see if you can check the last bowel movement to ensure it is firm.

Pick the puppy that exhibits the personality traits that you want in your dog. If you want a forward, friendly, excitable dog, the first puppy to greet you may be the one you seek. If you want a dog that will think things through and let others get more attention, look for a puppy who sits back and observes you before approaching.

CHAPTER 4
Preparing For Your Puppy

"To me it's most important to prepare your mindset, and then any changes needed in the home will be obvious. Think of what your expectations are long-term and decide what you will and won't allow. Do you want the adult dog to be sleeping on your bed, on the floor, or in a crate? Will you be allowing the adult dog on the couch? Aussiedoodles train very quickly, even as puppies, so be sure to hold them to that standard as soon as you bring them home."

Adrian Booher
Sunset Hill Farm

Photo Courtesy of
Kimberly Antolini

One of the most important things you will need to do before bringing your puppy home is to prepare your home. The first night in particular is going to be terrifying to the puppy, so you want to provide a safe and comfortable environment to help the pup get accustomed to the new home as quickly as possible. From puppy proofing the inside of your home and the yard to all of the supplies you need to buy, this is a time-intensive endeavor that is well worth the effort. Preparing a safe space with all of the essentials (especially the toys) will make the arrival of your newest family addition a great time for everyone – especially your new canine companion.

Preparing Your Kids

"If you have children be sure to talk to them about keeping small toys (legos especially!) out of reach of the new puppy."

Brey Sanchez
Marley's Doodles

You want your pup to feel comfortable from the beginning, which means making sure any children are careful and gentle when interacting with the new family member, whether the dog is a puppy or an adult. Begin to prepare your kids as soon as you plan to adopt your Aussiedoodle.

The following are the five golden rules that children should follow from the very first interaction.

1. Always be gentle.
2. Chase is an outside game.
3. Always leave the puppy alone during mealtime.
4. The Aussiedoodle should always remain firmly on the ground.
5. All of your valuables should be kept well out of the puppy's reach.

Since your kids are going to ask why, here are the explanations you can give them. You can simplify them for younger kids, or start a dialogue with teens.

Always Be Gentle

Little Aussiedoodle puppies are absolutely adorable, but all activities should be undertaken with a measure of caution, with all people holding back during play. It's very similar to playing with a toddler, so treat the playtime that way. This can be more difficult to teach younger children.

This rule must be applied consistently every time your children play with the puppy. Be firm if you see your children getting too excited or rough. You don't want the puppy to get overly excited either because he might end up nipping or biting. If he does, it isn't his fault because he hasn't learned better yet – it's the child's fault. Make sure your children understand the possible repercussions if they get too rough.

Chase

Running inside the home is dangerous for two primary reasons. It gives your Aussiedoodle puppy the impression that your home isn't safe inside because he is being chased. Or your puppy will learn that running inside is fine, which can be very dangerous as the dog gets older. One of the last things you want is for your Aussiedoodle to go barreling through your home knocking people off their feet because it was fine for him to run through the house when he was a puppy.

It can be easy for children to forget the rules as they start to play and everyone gets excited. That short game of getting away can quickly devolve into chase, so you will need to make sure your children understand not to start running. Once they get outside, chasing is perfectly fine (though you will still need to monitor the playtime).

Mealtime

Aussiedoodles are known for being loving and affectionate, so aggression really isn't something that you will likely see in your puppy. It isn't likely she will nip or bite because someone is near her food. However, your puppy can feel insecure about eating if she feels like someone may take her food away, which is obviously not fair to your Aussiedoodle. And older Aussiedoodles can be a bit more protective of its food, which could lead to some conflicts. Save yourself, your family, and your Aussiedoodle trouble by making sure everyone knows that eating time is your Aussiedoodle's time alone. Similarly, teach your kids that their own mealtime is off limits to the puppy. No feeding her from the table.

Paws On The Ground

No one should be picking the puppy up off the ground. You may want to carry your new family member around or play with the pup like a baby, but you and your family will need to resist that urge. Kids particularly have trouble understanding since they will see the Aussiedoodle puppy more like a toy than a living creature. The younger your children are, the more difficult it will be for them to understand the difference. It is so tempting to treat the Aussiedoodle like a baby and to try to carry it like one, but this is incredibly uncomfortable and unhealthy for the puppy. Older kids will quickly learn that a puppy nip or bite hurts a lot more than you would think. Those little teeth are incredibly sharp, and you don't want the puppy to be dropped. If your children learn never to pick up the puppy, things will go a lot better. Remember, this also applies to you, so don't make things difficult by doing something you constantly tell your children not to do.

Keep Valuables Out Of Reach

"Pick up your shoes and put them away. Anything left out on the floor is fair game for a new puppy, the floor is his world. He hasn't learned the rules yet so you can't punish him for your mistakes. If you leave your new baseball glove on the floor and the puppy uses it for a rawhide chew shame on YOU! It will take about a year before the puppy matures enough to be trusted and is trained well enough to leave things alone."

Kristine Robards
Double R Doodles

Valuables are not something you want to end up in the puppy's mouth, whether that's toys, jewelry, shoes, etc. Your kids will be less than happy if their personal possessions are chewed up by an inquisitive puppy, so teach them to put toys, clothes, and other valuables far out of the puppy's reach. Your Aussiedoodle may not be big yet, but you don't know how big that pup will be in a few months. It is best to get in the habit of keeping surfaces clear and valuables off the floor.

Photo Courtesy of Patrick Ruhl

You will need to be ready to refresh these rules regularly, both before the puppy arrives and after the arrival. The first time your kids begin to play with the puppy, you will need to be present, and you cannot leave them alone. Older teens will probably be all right to help with the puppy, but younger teens and kids should not be left alone with the puppy for a few months. Remember that you will need to be very firm with your kids to make sure that the puppy is not hurt or frightened.

Preparing Your Current Dogs

"Before deciding on a male or female give careful thought to other animals and people in your home. A female usually only bonds with one person (generally the main caregiver) and a male tends to bond with the whole family. If you already have a dog in your family it is usually best to purchase a puppy of the opposite sex for a second dog. Having said that, two neutered males will generally get along well with each other. Two spayed females can be 'ify'!"

Kristine Robards
Double R Doodles

Aussiedoodles are equal opportunity adorers – they love people and dogs equally. When they are puppies, you have a chance to start socializing them with your other dogs, but in most cases it is a fairly easy process, as long as your dog is all right with you bringing a puppy into the home.

If you already have canines in your home, they are going to need to be prepared for the new arrival. Here are the important tasks to prepare your current pets for your new arrival.

- Set a schedule for the things you will need to do and the people who will need to participate.

- Preserve your current dogs' favorite places and furniture, and make sure their toys and items are not in the puppy's space.

- Have play dates with other dogs at your home and analyze your dogs to see how they react.

Set A Schedule

Establish a schedule that you will keep once the puppy arrives. This lets your current furry companions know that they are still loved after a puppy arrives. Obviously, the puppy is going to get a lot of attention, so you need to make a concerted effort to let your current canine know that you still love and care for him. Basically, you are making time in your schedule just for your current dog or dogs, and you need to make sure that you don't stray from that schedule after the puppy's arrival.

Make sure that you plan to have at least one adult around for each other dog you have. Cats are generally less of a concern, but you will probably want to have at least one adult around when the puppy comes home. Aussiedoodles are a herding breed that may be inclined to chase smaller animals. To ensure your puppy doesn't terrorize your cat, you will need to make sure your cat has plenty of space to escape an overenthusiastic puppy. We will go into more detail later about what the roles of the other adults will be, but for now, when you know what date you will be bringing your puppy home, make sure that you have adults who know to be present to help. You may need to remind them as the time nears, so set an alert on your phone for that, as well as the date, time, and pickup information for your puppy.

One benefit of having a schedule for your other dogs in place before your Aussiedoodle puppy arrives is that it will be easy to keep a schedule with the puppy. Aussiedoodles love to know what to expect because both parent breeds were working dogs that generally worked on a schedule. Your other dogs can help you adapt to that so that you can better support your puppy from the beginning.

Your puppy is going to eat, sleep, and spend most of the day and night in his assigned space. This means that the space cannot block your current canine from his favorite furniture, bed, or any place where he rests over the course of the day. None of your current dog's stuff should be in this area, and this includes toys. You don't want your dog to feel like the puppy is taking over his territory. Make sure your children understand to never put your current dog's stuff in the puppy's area as well.

Your dog and the puppy will need to be kept apart in the early days, (even if they seem friendly) until your puppy has been fully vaccinated. Puppies are susceptible to illness, so wait until the puppy is protected before the dogs spend time together.

Getting An Idea How Your Dogs Will React – Extra At Home Playdates

Think about your dog's personality to help you decide the best way to prepare for that first day, week, and month. Each dog is unique, so you will need to consider your dog's personality to determine how things will go when the new dog arrives. Excitable dogs will need special attention to keep them from getting overly agitated when a new dog comes home. You don't want them to be so excited they accidentally hurt the new Aussiedoodle. Considering how playful your puppy may be, this can trigger excitement in some dogs, so make sure you have a plan in place to calm them down once the puppy arrives.

Consider the times when you have had other dogs in your home and how your current dog reacted to these other furry visitors. If your canine displayed territorial tendencies, or protective or possessive behavior, whether or toys or people, you will need to be extra careful with how you introduce your new pup. If you haven't invited another dog to your home, have a couple of play dates with other dogs at your home before your new Aussiedoodle arrives. You have to know how your current fur babies will react to new dogs in the house so you can properly prepare. Meeting a dog at home is very different from encountering one outside the home.

Food is one reason dogs display some kind of aggression because they don't want anyone trying to eat what is theirs. Just like people, you may find that when they are together your dogs act differently, which you will need to keep in mind as you plan their first introduction. See chapter 9 for planning to introduce your current dogs and your new puppy, and how to juggle a new puppy and your current pets.

Preparing A Puppy Space

"Aussiedoodles love to shred blankets or stuffed toys. If you get them fleece blankets they will hold up better than beds that have stuffing inside of them."

Mary Ann McGregor
Hearthside Country

Your puppy is going to need a dedicated space that includes a crate (you will need a small one in the beginning, but later you are going to need to upgrade to something bigger – or you can look into getting a crate that can be resized as your puppy grows), food and water bowls, pee pad, and toys. This will need to be in an area where the puppy will be when you are not able to give him dedicated attention. The puppy space should be safe and gated so that the puppy can't get out and young children and dogs can't get in. It should be a safe space where the puppy can see you going about your usual business and feel comfortable during the first night.

Dangerous Foods

Dogs can eat raw meat without having to worry about the kinds of problems a person will encounter. However, there are human foods that could be fatal to your Aussiedoodle. You should keep these foods away from all dogs:

- Apple seeds
- Chocolate
- Coffee
- Cooked bones (they can kill a dog when the bones splinter in the dog's mouth or stomach)
- Corn on the cob (the cob is deadly to dogs; corn off the cob is fine)
- Grapes/raisins
- Macadamia nuts
- Onions and chives
- Peaches, persimmons, and plums
- Tobacco (your Aussiedoodle will not know that it is not a food and may eat it if it's left out)
- Xylitol (a sugar substitute in candies and baked goods)
- Yeast

In addition to these potentially deadly foods, the Canine Journal has a lengthy list of foods that should be avoided.

Hazards to Fix

Preparing for a puppy is time consuming, and all of the most dangerous rooms and items in your home will be equally as dangerous to your puppy as they are to a baby. The biggest difference is that your Aussiedoodle is going to be mobile much faster than a child, potentially getting into dangerous situations within a few weeks if you don't eliminate all of the dangers ahead of your puppy's arrival.

Be aware that Aussiedoodles (puppies in general) will try to eat virtually anything, even if it isn't food. Nothing is safe – not even your furniture. Puppies will gnaw on wood and metal. Anything within their reach is fair game. Keep this in mind as you go about puppy-proofing your home.

Indoor Fixes

This section details the areas inside your home where you should really focus your attention. In case of problems, have your vet's number posted on the fridge and at least one other room in the house. If you set this up before your pup arrives, it will be there if you need it. Even if you program it into your phone, another family member or someone taking care of your Aussiedoodle may need the number.

Hazards	Fixes	Time Estimate
Kitchen		
Poisons	Keep in secured, childproof cabinets or on high shelves	30 min
Trash cans	Have a lockable trashcan, or keep it in a secured location	10 min
Appliances	Make sure all cords are out of reach	15 min
Human Food	Keep out of reach	Constant (start making it a habit)
Floors		
Slippery surfaces	Put down rugs or special mats designed to stick to the floor	30 min – 1 hour
Training area	Train on non-slippery surfaces	Constant
Bathrooms		
Toilet brush	Either have one that locks or keep out of reach	5 min/bathroom
Poisons	Keep in secured, childproof cabinets or on high shelves	15 - 30 min/ bathroom
Toilets	Keep closed Do not use automatic toilet cleaning chemicals	Constant (start making it a habit)
Cabinets	Keep locked with childproof locks	15 - 30 min/ bathroom
Laundry Room		
Clothing	Store clean and dirty clothing off the floor, out of reach	15 – 30 min
Poisons (bleach, pods/detergent, dryer sheets, and misc. poisons)	Keep in secured, childproof cabinets or on high shelves	15 min
Around the Home		
Plants	Keep off the floor	45 min – 1 hour
Trash cans	Have a lockable trashcan, or keep it in a secured location	30 min
Electrical cords, window blind cords	Hide them or makes sure they are out of reach; pay particular attention to entertainment and computer areas	1.5 hours

Poisons	Check to make sure there aren't any (WD40, window/screen cleaner, carpet cleaner, air fresheners); move all poisons to a centralized, locked location	1 hour
Windows	Check that cords are out of reach in all rooms	1 – 2 hours
Fireplaces	Store cleaning supplies and tools where the puppy can't get into them Cover the fireplace opening with something the puppy can't knock over	10 min/fireplace
Stairs	Cordon them off so that your puppy cannot try to go up or down them; make sure to test gates/blocks	10 – 15 min
Coffee tables/ End tables/ Nightstands	Clear them of dangerous objects (e.g., scissors, sewing equipment, pens, and pencils) and all valuables	30 – 45 min

If you have a cat, keep the litter box off the floor. It needs to be somewhere that your cat can easily go but your Aussiedoodle cannot. Since this involves teaching your cat to use the new area, it's something you should do well in advance of the puppy's arrival. You don't want your cat to undergo too many significant changes all at once. The puppy will be enough of a disruption – if your cat associates the litter box change with the puppy, you may find your cat protesting the change by refusing to use the litter box. Remember, you don't know how your Aussiedoodle is going to react to a cat, so give your kitty a place to escape to that is also comfortable.

Aussiedoodles can get into nearly everything at their height, and they will be exploring a lot when given the opportunity. Your Aussiedoodle is going to figure out how to do things you don't want her to do. This could range from getting into an open toilet (which is why you cannot have automatic-chemical rinses) to crawling into cabinets or pantries. As intelligent as the breed is, it's best to overestimate what your puppy can do and prepare accordingly. Get low and see each room from your Aussiedoodle's perspective. You are almost guaranteed to find at least one thing you missed.

Outdoor Fixes

This section details the things outside your home that need your attention ahead of your puppy's arrival. Also post the vet's number in one of the sheltered areas in case of an emergency.

Hazards	Fixes	Time Estimate
Garage		
Poisons	Keep in secured, childproof cabinets or on high shelves (e.g., car chemicals, cleaning, paint, lawn care) – this includes fertilizer	1 hour
Trash bins	Keep them in a secured location	5 min
Tools (e.g., lawn, car, hardware, power tools)	Make sure all cords are out of reach: Keep out of reach and never hanging over the side of surfaces	30 min – 1 hour
Equipment (e.g., sports, fishing)	Keep out of reach and never hanging over the side of surfaces	Constant (start making it a habit)
Sharp implements	Keep out of reach and never hanging over the side of surfaces	30 min
Bikes	Store off the ground or in a place the Aussiedoodle cannot get to (to keep the pup from biting the tires)	20 min
Fencing (Can Be Done Concurrently)		
Breaks	Fix any breaks in the fencing	30 min - 1 hour
Gaps	Fill any gaps, even if they are intentional, so your Aussiedoodle doesn't escape	30 min - 1 hour
Holes/Dips at Base	Fill any area that can be easily crawled under	1 – 2 hours
Yard		
Poisons	Don't leave any poisons in the yard	1 – 2 hours
Plants	Verify that all low plants aren't poisonous to dogs; fence off anything that is (such as grape vines)	45 min – 1 hour
Tools (e.g., lawn maintenance and gardening tools)	Make sure they are out of reach; Make sure nothing is hanging over outdoor tables	30 min – 1 hour

Never leave your Aussiedoodle alone in the garage, even as an adult. It's likely that your puppy will be in the garage when you take car trips, which is why it's important to puppy proof it. You should always have an eye on the dog, but you obviously can't climb under the car and will have a hard time getting into smaller spaces if your Aussiedoodle makes a break for it to explore – adult Aussiedoodles may be too big, but as puppies they are small enough to get into all kinds of tiny spaces.

Just like inside, you will need to follow up your outdoor preparations by getting low and checking out all areas from a puppy's perspective. Again, you are all but guaranteed to find at least one thing you missed.

Supplies And Tools To Purchase And Prepare

"Understanding puppy needs can minimize chewing and nipping problems. Their puppy teeth are going to be itchy, and their joints and muscles need stretching. If they have chew toys that they know are theirs and adequate opportunities to stretch, they will look to please you and be content."

Adrian Booher
Sunset Hill Farm

Photo Courtesy of
Isabel DeWitt

Photo Courtesy of Jessica Klaric

"Get toys that are appropriate for young puppies. They love ones with squeakers, and ones that have paper inside that make a rattley noise. Aussiedoodles also love balls to play with. They love for you to play with them. Get a sturdy food and water dish, and a nice pad to put under the food and water dish will be a big help in keeping that area clean."

Mary Ann McGregor
Hearthside Country

Planning for your puppy's arrival means buying a lot of supplies up front. You will need a wide range of items. If you start making purchases around the time you identify the breeder or rescue, you can stretch out your expenses over a longer period of time. This will make it seem a lot less expensive than it actually is, though an Aussiedoodle's needs are less expensive than what is required for most other breeds. The following are recommended items:

- Crate
- Bed
- Leash
- Doggie bags for walks
- Collar
- Tags
- Puppy food
- Water and food bowls (sharing a water bowl is usually okay, but your puppy needs her own food dish if you have multiple dogs)
- Toothbrush/Toothpaste
- Brush
- Toys
- Training treats

Health care items like flea treatments can be purchased, but they are expensive and you won't need them for a while. Puppies should not be treated until they reach a specified age. Talk to your vet before buying any medications.

For the crate, you only want to get one that is adequate for a puppy. Since you don't know how big your Aussiedoodle will get, you should avoid getting the crate for a larger dog so that you aren't buying three or four crates as your puppy grows to full size. If you decide to go with a crate that can be resized as your dog grows, you may not need to get another crate (if your dog stays on the smaller side of medium). If your dog grows to be on the larger side, you will need a new crate, but at least you will be able to resize it for the first half year or so, helping to keep your pup comfortable instead of feeling cramped.

Choosing Your Vet

Photo Courtesy of Christine Riesser

Whether you get a puppy or an adult, you should take your canine to the vet within 48 hours (24 hours is strongly recommended) of her arrival. Getting an appointment with a vet can take a while, just like getting a doctor's appointment, so you will need to have your vet and the first appointment booked well in advance.

Here are some things to consider when looking for a vet.

• What is their level of familiarity with Aussiedoodles? They don't have to be specialists, but you do want them to have some experience with the breed.

• How far from your home is the vet? You don't want the vet to be more than 30 minutes away in case of emergency.

• Is the vet available for emergencies after hours or can they recommend a vet in case of an emergency?

• Is the vet part of a local vet hospital if needed, or does the doctor refer patients to a local pet hospital?

• Is the vet the only vet or one of several partners? If he or she is part of a partnership, can you stick with just one vet for visits?

• How are appointments booked?

• Can you have other services performed there, such as grooming and boarding?

• Is the vet accredited?

• What are the prices for the initial visit and the normal costs, such as shots and regular visits?

• What tests and checks are performed during the initial visit?

Make time to visit the vet you are considering using so that you can look around to see what the environment is like inside the office. See if you can speak to the vet to see if he or she is willing to help put you at ease and answer your questions. A vet's time is valuable, but they should have a few minutes to help you feel confident that they are the right choice to help take care of your canine.

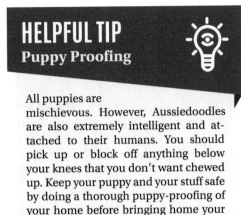

HELPFUL TIP
Puppy Proofing

All puppies are mischievous. However, Aussiedoodles are also extremely intelligent and attached to their humans. You should pick up or block off anything below your knees that you don't want chewed up. Keep your puppy and your stuff safe by doing a thorough puppy-proofing of your home before bringing home your Aussiedoodle puppy.

Planning The First Year's Budget

Begin establishing a monthly budget the day you decide to get your puppy. The cost will include the adoption cost, which is typically higher for a designer dog than for a rescue. Of course there are some items that are one-time purchases, such as water and food bowls, but many other items will need to be purchased regularly, like food and treats. The vet and other healthcare costs should be included in your budget. Regular vaccinations are required, and an annual checkup should be included in the budget.

If you want to join an Aussiedoodle organization, budget for that. There are a lot of things you can do with Aussiedoodles if you want to be with other puppy parents. Taking the time to train with other dogs is advised for the Aussiedoodle because they need as much positive socialization as possible in the early days. Taking classes with other dogs helps familiarize your puppy with other dogs in a safe environment. More details will be provided in a later chapter; for now it is important to budget this extra expense so that you can get your pup the socialization needed to help make her comfortable around other dogs.

The following table can help you start to plan your budget. Keep in mind that the prices are a rough average, and may be significantly different based on where you live.

Item	Considerations	Estimated Costs
Crate	This should be a comfortable space where the puppy will sleep and rest.	Wire crates: Range $60 to $350 Portable crate: Range $35 to $200
Bed	This will be placed in the crate.	$10 to $55
Leash	It should be short in the beginning because you need to be able to keep your puppy from getting over-excited and running to the end of a long line.	Short leash: $6 to $15 Retract-able: $8 to $25
Doggie bags for walks	It's best to purchase packs to ensure you don't run out of bags.	Singles cost less than $1 each. Packs: $4 to $16
Collar	You will likely need two types: one for the puppy, and one for an adult Aussiedoodle. Hold off on buying the second until closer to the end of the year when you have an idea of how big the dog will be. Your Aussie-doodle will not be full sized yet, but will likely need a new collar by then.	$10 to $30
Tags	These will likely be provided by your vet. Find out what information the vet provides for tags, then purchase any tags that are not provided. At a minimum, your Aussiedoodle should have tags with your address on it in case the pup escapes.	Contact your vet be-fore purchasing to see if the required rabies tags include your contact info.
Puppy food	This one is going to depend on if you make your Aussiedoodle food, if you purchase food, or both. The larger the bag, the higher the cost, but the fewer times you will need to purchase food. You will need to purchase puppy specific food in the beginning, but will stop after the second year. Adult dog food is more expensive.	$9 to $90 per bag
Water and food bowls	If you have other dogs, you will need separate bowls for the puppy.	$10 to $40

Toothbrush/ Toothpaste	You will need to brush regularly, so plan to use more than one tooth-brush during the first year.	$2.50 t0 $14
Brush	Aussiedoodle coats are incredibly easy to maintain, but you should still brush them regularly. When they are puppies, brushing offers a great way to bond.	$3.50 to $20
Toys	You definitely want to get your puppy toys, and you are going to want toys for more aggressive chewers, even if your puppy goes through them remarkably quickly. You will want to keep getting your Aussiedoodle toys as an adult (cost of adult dog toys not included).	$2.00 Packs of toys range from $10 to $20 (easier in the long run as your pup will chew through toys quickly)
Training treats	You will need those from the beginning, and likely won't need to change the treats based on your Aussiedoodle's age; you may need to change treats to keep your dog's interest though.	$4.50to $15

You won't need to purchase the adult version of these items before the puppy arrives, but you will probably need them by the end of the year. Set up a budget for the initial costs, then a second budget for adult versions of items that will need to be replaced as the puppy grows. You will have the better part of a year to purchase them, but it will sneak up fast.

CHAPTER 5
Bringing Home Your Aussiedoodle

Bringing an Aussiedoodle home can be absolutely incredible, but it also means being prepared to start training your pooch as soon as the puppy enters your care. As with any intelligent breed, you'll need to start training your pup right from the beginning, even if you are rescuing an adult dog. They may have a great temperament and personality, but there is a reason why it may not be a good idea to have an Aussiedoodle be a family's first dog – they can be stubborn and insist on having things their own way. You should prepare for this possibility, then be pleasantly surprised if your pooch ends up being more like a Poodle.

There are a lot of similarities between bringing home a puppy and a newborn, with the primary difference being that the puppy is already mobile and learning. That puppy is going to require a lot more than changing, feeding, and cuddling; however, it will be more than worth it in the end.

Photo Courtesy of
Dan Oltersdorf

Photo Courtesy of
Trista Caudill

Final Preparations And Planning

Intelligent dogs like the Aussiedoodle, require that you be around for the whole first week and as much of the first month as possible. To do this, you may need to take time off from work or negotiate working from home during at least the first 24 hours, if not the first 48 hours. The more time you can dedicate in those first few days, the better for your new family member.

Start creating a list as you begin your search for a puppy or adult. You've already seen that there are a lot of preparations that need to be made, but preparing the house is just one of the important tasks. The following are some useful checklists to get you through the preparation for your puppy and the aftermath of his arrival at your home.

Puppy Supplies To Get Before Your Aussiedoodle Arrives

The following are essentials to have in place before your puppy arrives, to avoid having to run to the store in a panic when you realize you're missing something.

- Food
- Bed
- Crate
- Toys
- Water and food dishes
- Leash
- Collar
- Treats
- Training schedule and tools

All of these items should be set up and ready for use before the puppy arrives. They are largely going to be stored in the puppy's space, which should make it a little easier to verify that you have all of the necessary supplies during the final check.

Pre-Arrival Home Inspection

No matter how busy you are, you need to take the time to inspect the home one more time before the puppy arrives. Set aside an hour or two to complete this a day or two before the puppy arrives.

A Tentative Puppy Schedule

Prepare a tentative schedule to help you get started over the course of the week. Your days are about to get very busy, so you need somewhere to start before your puppy arrives. Use the information from Set a Schedule to get started, but make sure you do this earlier instead of later.

Initial Meeting

Have a meeting with all of the family members to make sure all of the rules discussed in Chapter 4 are remembered and understood before the puppy is a distraction. This includes how to handle the puppy. Determine who is going to be responsible for primary puppy care, including who will be the primary trainer. To help teach younger children about responsibility, a parent can pair with a child to manage the puppy's care. The child will be responsible for things like keeping the water bowl filled and feeding the puppy, while a parent oversees the tasks.

The Ride Home

"When you pick up your new Aussiedoodle from the breeder, take a crate, puppy pads or news papers for the crate, wet ones, paper towels, a garbage bag, dish for water, and a bottle of water. On the way home NEVER stop and put your puppy out on the ground, especially at a rest area. This is an excellent way to expose him to the Parvo Virus, he is not fully vaccinated yet, do not do this. Rather let him use the crate, then immediately clean it, or put puppy pads or news papers on the floor of the car or back of the SUV and let him run around for a few minutes and do his business there, just don't put him on the ground until you get home."

Kristine Robards
Double R Doodles

As tempting as it is to cuddle and try to make the ride comfortable, using a crate for the ride home is both safer and more comfortable for the puppy.

Before leaving your home, make sure you have everything you need prepared.

- The crate should be anchored for safety and include a cushion.
- Call to make sure everything is still on schedule and make sure the puppy is ready.
- Ask, if you haven't already, if you can get the mother to leave her scent on a blanket to help make the puppy's transition more comfortable.
- Make sure your other adult remembers and will be on time to head to the pickup destination.
- If you have other dogs, make sure that all of the adults involved know what to do and where to go for that first neutral meeting.

Two adults should be present on the first trip. Ask the breeder if the puppy has been in a car before, and, if not, it is especially important to have someone who can give the puppy attention while the other person drives. The puppy will be in the crate, but someone can still provide comfort. It will definitely be scary because the puppy no longer has mom, siblings, or known people around, so having someone present to talk to the puppy will make it less of an ordeal for the little guy.

Photo Courtesy of
Jaime Matkowsky

This is the time to start teaching your puppy that car trips are enjoyable. This means making sure that the crate is secure. You don't want to terrify the puppy by letting the crate slide around while the puppy is helpless inside. This kind of jostling will teach your canine that cars are terrifying instead of making them feel safe.

First Night Frights

"I recommend a floor fan that only blows partially on the puppies crate so he or she can get out of the air if they get chilled. The fan is also great white noise to help the puppy to sleep!"

Pam Keith
Doodles Galore

That first night is going to be scary to your little Aussiedoodle puppy. As understandable as this may be, there is only so much comfort you can give your new family member. Just like with a baby, the more you respond to cries and whimpering, the more you are teaching a puppy that negative behaviors will provide the desired results. You will need to be prepared for a balancing act to provide reassurance that things will be all right while keeping your puppy from learning that crying gets your attention.

Create a sleeping area just for your puppy near where you sleep. The area should have the puppy's bed tucked safely into a crate. It offers him a safe place to hide so that he can feel more comfortable in a strange new home. The entire area should be blocked off so that no one can get into it (and the puppy can't get out) during the night. It should also be close to where people sleep so that the puppy doesn't feel abandoned. If you were able to get a blanket or pillow that smells like the mother, make sure this is in your puppy's space. Consider adding a little white noise to cover unfamiliar sounds that could scare your new pet.

Your puppy will make noises over the course of the night. Don't move the puppy away, even if the whimpering keeps you awake. If you give in, over time the whimpering, whining, and crying will get louder. Spare yourself some trouble later by teaching the puppy that it won't work. Being moved away from people will only scare the puppy more, reinforcing the anxiety. Over time, simply being close

HELPFUL TIP
A Big Adjustment

The first few days in your home will be a big adjustment for your Aussiedoodle puppy. He'll have just left his mom, littermates, and the only home he's ever known. He'll be in a new place with new rules and (maybe) other pets. Understand that your puppy may be overwhelmed and could react by having more or less energy than usual or by being very vocal.

to you at night will be enough to reassure your puppy that everything will be all right.

Losing sleep is part of the deal of bringing a puppy into your home. Fortunately, it doesn't take as long to get a puppy acclimated as it takes with a human infant, so your normal schedule can resume more quickly.

Don't let your puppy into your bed that first night – or any other night – until he is fully housetrained. Once an Aussiedoodle learns that the bed is accessible, you can't train him not to hop on it. If he isn't housetrained, you'll need a new bed in the very near future.

Whatever housetraining path you use, you are going to need to keep to a schedule, even during the night to train your puppy where to use the bathroom. Puppies will need to go to the bathroom every two to three hours, and you will need to get up during the night to make sure your puppy understands that he is to always go to the bathroom either outside or on the pee pad. If you let it go at night, you are going to have a difficult time training him that he cannot go in the house later.

Photo Courtesy of
Carolina Cantieri

First Vet Visit

"Only vaccinate with the four-combo core vaccines and never the 5-combo. I've had puppies on the verge of a painful death from reaction to the five-combo. Also, be cautious with heartworm medication. Ask a knowledgeable veterinarian about which heartworm medication is appropriate. Not all veterinarians know about these cautions."

Sheron MW Steele, PhD
XANADU of the Rockies

A vet's visit is necessary within the first day or two of your puppy's arrival and may be required in the contract you signed with a breeder. You need to establish a baseline for the puppy's health so that the vet can track progress and monitor the puppy to ensure everything is going well as your Aussiedoodle grows. It also creates a rapport between your Aussiedoodle and the vet, which can help too. The initial assessment gives you more information about your puppy, as well as giving you a chance to ask the vet questions and get advice.

Wanting to explore and greet everyone and everything is going to be something that your puppy is very likely to want to do at the vet's office. Both people and other pets are likely to attract your puppy's attention. This is a chance for you to work on socializing the puppy, though you will need to be careful. Always ask the person if it is all right for your puppy to meet any other pet, and wait for approval before letting your puppy move forward with meeting other animals. Pets at the vet's office are very likely to not be feeling great, which means they may not be very affable. You don't want a grumpy older dog or a sick animal to nip, hurt, or scare your puppy. Nor do you want your puppy to be exposed to anything potentially dangerous while still getting his shots. You want the other animal to be happy about the meeting (though not too excited) so that it is a positive experience for your puppy.

Having a positive first experience with other animals can make the visit to see the vet less of a scary experience, and something that your Aussiedoodle can enjoy, at least a little. This can help your puppy feel more at ease during the visits.

If you already have a vet, take a few minutes to ask about her experience with the breed. Considering how over-energetic Australian Shepherds

Photo Courtesy of
Jessica Klaric

can be, some vets may have had some interesting experiences with them. They may want to herd other animals in the vet if they are overexcited or under-exercised. Vets aren't likely to turn you away your dog, but you may want to see if there is anything in the vet that could help, or if you should bring something along (if your dog takes after the Australian Shepherd side).

You want to find a vet that is fairly close to your home, usually within a few miles, so if your puppy gets sick or injured, you can get to the vet's office quickly.

During the first visit, the vet will conduct an initial assessment of your Aussiedoodle. One of the most important things the vet will do is take your puppy's weight. This is something you are going to have to monitor for your Aussiedoodle's entire life because the breed is prone to obesity. Record the weight for yourself so you can see how quickly the puppy is growing. Ask your vet what a healthy weight is at each stage, and record that as well. Aussiedoodles should be growing unbelievably fast during that first year, but you should still make sure your Aussiedoodle isn't gaining more weight than is healthy.

The vet will set up the date for the next set of shots, which will likely happen not too long after your puppy arrives. When it is time for his vaccination, be prepared for a day or two of your puppy feeling under the weather.

The Start Of Training

"Be the boss and do not allow nipping and jumping as a puppy. It can be cute one time and the next it's not. It's harder to break the older they get."

Donna Molitor
DoncieDoodles

As mentioned, training starts from the moment your Aussiedoodle becomes your responsibility, and that will be true for the entire life of your pooch. Considering the fact that your dog may be stubborn, you want to start getting your pup used to the idea that you are in charge. This will help play against any stubbornness from the Australian Shepherd side. And if your dog takes more after the Poodle parent, it will be that much easier to train since he will be more inclined to listen.

The focus during these first few weeks is to start housetraining and minimize undesirable behavior, especially toward other animals, and feelings of being territorial. Training from the start is vital, but don't take your new puppy to any classes just yet. Most puppies have not had all of the necessary shots, and good trainers will not allow them in classes until the full first round of shots is complete.

Photo Courtesy of
Lindsey Kniceley

CHAPTER 6
The First Month

Photo Courtesy of Emily Devlieger

The first week is easily the most difficult time with your puppy, but keep in mind that your Aussiedoodle needs comfort, attention, and to feel a sense of belonging. The bond you start to build in that first week will develop over the first month. By the end of the month, your pup should be sleeping through the night and may have a fairly good understanding of where to go to the bathroom (though it is going to take you more than a month to have a fully housetrained Aussiedoodle). You will also have a pretty good understanding of your canine's personality.

The first month is when you really need to start paying attention to the emerging personality characteristics. You will need to work to stop or reduce any undesirable behaviors, particularly nipping, without being overbearing. Aussiedoodles respond very well to positive reinforcement, which means you should avoid punishments. This may be a bit more difficult in the early part of the month when you are still suffering from sleep deprivation, but you will need to try to keep it in mind so that the training is effective.

The key during this time is to remain consistent. As long as you stick to the rules, you will start seeing results quickly because both of the original breeds are intelligent and can understand what you mean much faster than the average dog. Use what you learn about your puppy's personality to encourage good behavior. Incorporating what you have learned over that first month is going to prove to be a boon because as your Aussiedoodle starts to bond with you, his instinct to work with you is going to start to really show.

Not Up To Full Strength – Don't Overdo It In The First Month

A tired puppy is a lot like a tired toddler; you have to keep the little guy from getting exhausted or overworking those little legs. Your pup is probably going to think that sleep is unnecessary, no matter how tired he is. It is up to you to read the signs to know when to stop all activities and put your pup to bed.

Be careful that you aren't pushing the training past the puppy's concentration threshold. If you continue training past your puppy's energy levels, the lessons learned are not going to be the ones you want to teach your dog. At this age, training sessions don't need to be long, they just need to be consistent.

Walks will be much shorter during that first month. When you do go out for walks, stay within a few blocks of home. Don't worry – by the month's end, your puppy will have a lot more stamina so you can enjoy longer walks and short trips away from home if needed. By the end of the first year you should be able to go for a short jog, depending on advice from your vet. You can do a bit of running on the leash in the yard if your puppy has a good bit of extra energy. This will help your Aussiedoodle learn how to behave on the leash while running. Puppies have a tendency to want to attack the leash because it is a distraction from running freely.

Just because your puppy can't take long walks doesn't mean that he won't have plenty of energy. Daily exercise will be essential, just with the caveat that you need to make sure your puppy isn't doing too much. Remember, he is from two intelligent breeds, which means he will get in trouble when he gets bored – and if he has those habits as an adult, you will have difficulties trying to get him to stop those undesirable behaviors, like chewing on furniture and jumping on people when he is excited. Staying active will help him to not only be healthy, but keep him mentally stimulated. You will quickly realize just how sedentary you have been if you have never had a dog before because you will be on the move almost all of the time the puppy is awake.

HELPFUL TIP
Socialization, Training, and Learning the Rules

The first month home with your Aussiedoodle puppy should be all about teaching him basic commands, teaching him the rules of your home, and exposing him to a variety of people, pets, and places. That will help him grow up to be happy, confident, and free of anxiety.

Setting The Rules And Sticking To Them

"Aussiedoodles need an authority figure, so be prepared to be firm and consistent with your demands. If they don't understand how to please you and what you expect of them, they will develop anxious behaviors, like chewing your personal items or barking inappropriately."

Adrian Booher
Sunset Hill Farm

Photo Courtesy of
Virginia Scallion

Photo Courtesy of
Oliver & Cristina Hinton

Your puppy needs to understand the rules and know that you and your family mean them. If you don't remain consistent, you are setting yourself and your Aussiedoodle up for a lot of contention, especially if your pup takes after the Australian Shepherd parent.

A firm, consistent approach is best for both of you. To ensure you both have fun, you have to make sure your puppy listens. Once your canine learns to listen to you, training your Aussiedoodle to do tricks can easily become a highlight to your day.

Treats And Rewards Vs. Punishments

A later chapter will go into details about training, but it is important to keep in mind just how much more efficient it is to train with rewards than with punishments. This will be a particular challenge as puppies can be exuberant and are easily distracted. It is important to remember that your puppy is young, so you need to keep your temper and learn when you need to take a break from training.

73

Separation Anxiety

"An Aussiedoodle is going to want to be with you 24/7. As a herding dog they are genetically geared to watch over their family. They should NEVER be on a chain, or outdoors alone, for any reason. If that is the temperament you are looking for, then an Aussiedoodle is not the breed for you. The up-side is that they are not prone to run off if let out of the yard, or when you go on a hike."

Joyce Wallace
Pecan Place Aussiedoodles

Australian Shepherds and Toy Poodles are generally classed as breeds with pretty substantial separation anxiety. Standard Poodles may not be quite as bad, but all working dogs are more likely to have separation anxiety. Working-dog separation anxiety is a bit different than toy breed anxiety. If you give your working dog something to do while you are gone, the separation won't be quite so intense; they mostly just get bored. Still, it is a problem that you are likely to encounter, so you need to plan to help your puppy understand that your being gone doesn't mean you won't return.

Photo Courtesy of
Cheri Karttunen

In the beginning, keep the puppy's time alone to a minimum. The sounds of people around the house will help your Aussiedoodle understand that the separation is not permanent. After the first week or so, the alone time can involve you going out to get the mail, leaving the puppy inside alone for just a few minutes. You can then lengthen the amount of time you are away from the puppy over a few days until the puppy is alone for 30 minutes or so at a time.

Here are some basic guidelines for when you start to leave your puppy alone.

- Take the puppy out about 30 minutes before you leave.
- Tire the puppy out with exercise or playtime so that your leaving is not such a big deal.
- Place the puppy in the puppy area well ahead of when you go out to avoid associating the space with something bad happening.
- Don't give your puppy extra attention right before you leave because that reinforces the idea that you give attention before something bad happens.
- Avoid reprimanding your Aussiedoodle for any behavior while you are away. This teaches him to be more stressed because it will seem like you come home angry.

If your Aussiedoodle exhibits signs of separation anxiety, there are several things you can do to help make him comfortable during your absence.

- Chew toys can give your puppy something acceptable to gnaw on while you are away.
- A blanket or shirt that smells like you or other family members can help provide comfort too. Just make sure you don't give your puppy dirty clothing while you are away.
- Leave the area well lit, even if it is during the day. Should something happen and you get home later than intended, you don't want your Aussiedoodle to be in the dark.
- Turn on a stereo (classical music is best) or television (old-timey shows that don't have loud noises, like Mr. Ed or I Love Lucy) so that the house isn't completely quiet and unfamiliar noises are less obvious.

Since they are a smart breed, it is not going to take your Aussiedoodle long to notice the kind of behaviors that indicate you are leaving. Grabbing your keys, purse, wallet, and other indications will quickly become triggers that can make your Aussiedoodle anxious. Don't make a big deal out of it. If you act normal, over time this will help your Aussiedoodle to understand that your leaving is fine and that everything will be all right.

Training Areas To Start During The First Month

"Aussiedoodles are very easy to train. Our advice is to take the time to do the training. Aussiedoodles want to know what is expected of them. Make sure that the rules you want them to follow as an adult dog are the same ones you start with from the very beginning."

Mary Ann McGregor
Hearthside Country

Training is covered in a later chapters, but there are several critical aspects that you will need to start during the first month:

- Housetraining
- Crate training
- Chewing
- Barking
- Protection (you won't start this during the first month, but you will need to start gauging for it if you want your dog to be an ideal protector)

You need to find out how much the breeder did in housetraining and other areas. The best breeders may even have puppies listening to one or two commands before they go home with you. If this is the case (and it is easier to do with Aussiedoodles), you will want to keep using those commands with your puppy so that the training is not lost. This can help you establish the right tone to use as the puppy will already know what the words mean and how to react to them. Once he understands that, he will more quickly pick up on other uses of that tone as the way you talk when you are training. It is another great way to let your little love know when you mean business versus when you want to play. These kinds of distinctions are easily picked up by Aussiedoodles and your dog will be more than happy to oblige.

Adopt a No Nipping Policy

"Aussiedoodles can nip, or herd, if not redirected and taught how to handle their natural tendencies. I redirect with training to fetch. And, it's very important to teach children to 'stop' and not participate if the puppy is trying to herd them. Aussiedoodles do not chase a non moving object."

Joyce Wallace
Pecan Place Aussiedoodles

All puppies nip, but breeds like the Aussiedoodle require more attention because of their extensive history on the shepherding side. Part of managing cattle is nipping at them and keeping them in line. This is why it is so critical to stop nipping behavior with an Aussiedoodle.

Some of the triggers for nipping are overstimulation, which can be one of the signs that your puppy is too tired to keep playing or training and you should put the pup to bed.

Another trigger could be that your canine has too much energy. If this is the case, you need to get your puppy outside for exercise to burn off some of that energy.

Obedience training is the best way to learn how to deal with nipping. Since puppies may not be ready for that kind of training in the first month, you need to be more aware and immediately let your puppy know that nipping is not acceptable. Some people recommend using a water spritzer bottle and spraying the puppy while saying "No" after nipping. This is one of the few times when punishment may be effective, but you need to be careful not to associate it with anything other than the nipping.

Always tell your puppy "No" firmly whenever there is nipping, even if it is during playtime. You should also pull away and say "Ouch!" loudly to let your puppy know that his teeth are hurting you. This will help to establish the idea that nipping is bad and is never rewarded.

Photo Courtesy of Briana Gaines

CHAPTER 7
Housetraining

"For the first few days, be extra vigilant to get to know their cues and responses. Unless you are directly engaged with your puppy, put them on a short leash beside you or confined to a crate. They will understand quickly what your expectations are if you have a consistent potty area in the yard. Take a few days off if you want to get it right from the start."

Adrian Booher
Sunset Hill Farm

Easily one of the worst parts of bringing a puppy into the home, housetraining is unpleasant and tries your patience. It is messy and requires you to keep your cool when your puppy doesn't seem to understand quite what you want. Despite how difficult it is, you have to keep your patience to get the point of the training across.

Keep in mind that potty training a toddler is just as trying, and it typically takes longer, so if you do it right, housetraining a puppy will be a good bit

Photo Courtesy of Kimberly Antolini

Photo Courtesy of Amy Johnson

easier. Unlike with a toddler though, you pretty much have to be in monitoring mode during the first few months (even if you have a yard). This is why it is so important to set a schedule and then not deviate from it.

Using a leash can be very helpful in ensuring that your puppy learns when and where to go, but there will still be challenges as you work to establish the hierarchy and convince your puppy to listen to you.

Make sure to consistently apply these two rules.

1. Never let the puppy roam the home alone. Dogs don't like having a dirty bed, so your pup is much less likely to have accidents in the crate or near his bedding. Your Aussiedoodle won't be pleased with the idea of being in a soiled crate, so that is a deterrent from using the bathroom when you are not around.

2. Give your puppy constant, easy access to the locations where you plan to housetrain. You will need to make frequent trips outside as your puppy learns where to do his business, particularly if constant access to a place to use the restroom isn't possible. When you go out, put a leash

Photo Courtesy of
Kristin-Annie Espinoza

on your puppy to make sure you make a point of where in the yard you want him to use the bathroom.

Always begin with a training plan, then be even stricter with yourself than you are with your puppy to keep that schedule. You are the key to the puppy learning where it is acceptable to do his business.

Inside Or Outside – Potty Training Options

If your breeder has already started housetraining the puppy, stick to the method that was used. Changing it will make your Aussiedoodle more likely to either get confused or to believe that housetraining is optional.

Your Housetraining Options And Considerations

Here are your options when it comes to housetraining your puppy:

- Pee pads – you should have several around the home for training, including in the puppy's area, but as far from the bed as possible
- Regular outings outside – set the schedule based on your puppy's sleeping and eating schedule
- Rewards – this can be treats in the beginning, but should quickly shift to praise

There are several factors that will influence how you begin training, particularly the weather outside. If the weather is too cold or hot, stick with training your puppy inside. He will not be likely to focus if he is too uncomfortable.

In the beginning the best way to housetrain is by going out a lot of times, including at night, so that your puppy learns to keep all business outside. During the first few months, it is best to use a leash when you take the puppy out. This allows you to help him learn to walk on a leash and keeps him from getting distracted.

A word of warning – don't start praising the puppy until the puppy is done going to the bathroom. Interrupting mid-potty may make the puppy stop, increasing the odds that your puppy will go again when you get back inside.

Setting A Schedule And Outdoor Restroom Location

"A crate is a must. Your puppy should be in the crate more then out when potty training. Know which door you will use for the potty training and keep it consistent. Your puppy will be as good as the time and effort you put into training."

Donna Molitor
DoncieDoodles

You need to keep an eye on your puppy and have housetraining sessions after several key activities:

- After eating
- After waking up from sleeping or naps
- On a schedule (after it has been established)

Photo Courtesy of
Gina Teague

Watch your Aussiedoodle for cues like sniffing and circling, two very common activities as a puppy searches for a place to go. Start tailoring your schedule around your puppy's unique needs.

Puppies have small bladders and little control in the early days. If you have to train your pup to go inside, there needs to be a single designated space with a clean pee pad in the puppy area, and you need to stock up on the appropriate pads for the puppy to have somewhere to go that isn't the floor. The pads are better than newspaper and can absorb more. You will need to plan to transition to outdoors as quickly as possible before the Aussiedoodle learns that doing his business inside is acceptable.

A designated restroom space can help make the experience easier. The Aussiedoodle will begin to associate one area of the yard for one purpose. When you get there, the expectation will be easier to understand faster than if you let the puppy sniff around and go anywhere in the yard. Having him go to one spot regularly will not only make training easier, but cleanup will be much simpler too; that way you can continue to use the whole yard instead of having to worry about stepping in waste whenever you or anyone else goes outside.

When out for walks is the perfect time to train your puppy to go. Between walks and the yard, your puppy will come to see the leash as a sign that it is time to relieve the bladder, which could become a Pavlovian response. Given that Aussiedoodles are so smart, it won't take your companion long to understand the correlation either.

Make sure that you pay attention to your puppy the entire time you are outside. You need to make sure that the puppy understands the purpose of going outside is to go to the bathroom. That means he has to go while you are outside. Do not send your puppy outside and assume that he's done what you wanted him to do. Until there are no more accidents in the home, you need to verify that your puppy isn't losing focus while he is outside.

Key Words

All training should include key words, even housetraining. You and all members of the family should know what words to use when training your dog where to go to the bathroom, and you should all be using those words consistently. If you have paired an adult with a child, the adult should be the one using the keyword during training.

Be careful not to select words that you often use inside the home because you don't want to confuse your puppy. Use a phrase like "Get busy" to let your puppy know it's time to get to work. It's not a phrase most people use in their daily routine, so it is not something you are likely to say when you don't mean for your puppy to use the bathroom.

Once your puppy learns to use the bathroom based on the command, make sure he finishes before offering praise or rewards.

Positive Reinforcement – Rewarding Good Behavior

"He will begin to wander off to look for a secluded place to go, he may begin to circle, we call this the 'puppy poo poo dance', pick him up take him outside, always use the same door, go to the same spot in the yard, put him down, when he starts to go, say 'Go Potty' then be a cheerleader, clap your hands, be excited, say good boy, make sure he's finished, give him a treat and take him inside."

Kristine Robards
Double R Doodles

Positive reinforcement is unbelievably effective with Aussiedoodles. In the beginning, take a few pieces of kibble with you when you are teaching your puppy where to go, both inside and outside. Learning that you are the one in charge will help teach the Aussiedoodle to look to you for cues and instructions.

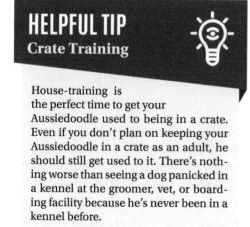

HELPFUL TIP
Crate Training

House-training is the perfect time to get your Aussiedoodle used to being in a crate. Even if you don't plan on keeping your Aussiedoodle in a crate as an adult, he should still get used to it. There's nothing worse than seeing a dog panicked in a kennel at the groomer, vet, or boarding facility because he's never been in a kennel before.

While you are being firm and consistent, when your puppy does the right thing you also have to lavish the little guy with praise. If you gently lead your puppy to the area on a leash without any other stops, it will become obvious over time that your Aussiedoodle should go there to use the bathroom. Once you get outside, encourage your Aussiedoodle to go once you get to the place in the yard where you want him to go. In the beginning, this probably won't take too long, and as soon as he does his business, give him immediate and very enthusiastic praise. Pet your puppy as

Photo Courtesy of
Terhya Nyegaard
North Ridge Doodles

you talk to let the little guy know just how good the action was. Once the praise is done, return inside immediately. This is not playtime, so do not remain outside. You want your puppy to associate certain outings with designated potty time.

Praise is far more effective for Aussiedoodles, but you can give your puppy a treat after a few successful trips outside. Definitely do not make treats a habit after each trip because you do not want your Aussiedoodle to expect it every time. The last thing you want is for your Aussiedoodle to learn that this is all about treats. The lesson is to go outside, and that may include treats when it is done consistently.

The best way to train in that first month or two is to go out every hour or two, even at night. You will need to set an alarm to wake you within that time to take the puppy outside. Use the leash to keep the focus on using the bathroom, give the same enthusiastic praise, then immediately return inside and go to bed. It is incredibly difficult, but your Aussiedoodle will get the hang of it a lot faster if there isn't a long period between potty breaks. Over time, the pup will need to go out less frequently, giving you more rest.

If your Aussiedoodle has an accident, it is important to refrain from punishing the puppy. Accidents are not a reason to punish – it really reflects more on your training and schedule than what the puppy has learned. That said, accidents are pretty much an inevitability. When it happens, tell your puppy, "No. Potty outside!" and clean the mess immediately. Once that is done take the puppy outside to go potty. Of course, if your puppy doesn't go, he doesn't get any praise.

CHAPTER 8
Socialization And Experience

"The main socializing for a herding dog is to expose them to children when they are very young. The running and screaming that is typical with kids is stressful for a herding dog if they aren't exposed to it early on. I recommend that my buyers take their puppies to a soccer game to see families and kids if they don't have any of their own."

Joyce Wallace
Pecan Place Aussiedoodles

Aussiedoodles tend to be lovers and not fighters. Whether they are meeting new people, dogs, or other animals, they tend to be excited about the encounter; not wary or suspicious. For every breed, the best time to start socializing is between week 3 and 12.

Your puppy will need to have all of the necessary vaccinations before being exposed to other dogs, but that happens fairly early in your puppy's life. Once that's done, you can start making playdates with friends and their dogs. In the meantime, you can start introducing your dog to new people at least.

Photo Courtesy of
Karine Dolce

*Photo Courtesy of
Ashley LeMaster*

Socialization Is Easy But Still Important For Aussiedoodles

Since this is a breed that loves people and dogs, socialization is fairly easy. Their intelligence means that what you teach them in those first few trips outside will already start to make your puppy feel more comfortable when going out. Aussiedoodles usually love being with people and dogs, so there is already a lot to work with – mostly you are encouraging their natural temperament by providing a safe and friendly environment. As your Aussiedoodle ages, you will be able to do more and experience a much wider variety of adventures. However, in those early days, you want to keep the socialization of your pooch manageable (instead of overwhelming) and the environment predictable.

You will be responsible for ensuring that the people who want to interact with your young pooch understand how to play responsibly with your newest family member. This is particularly true when it comes to picking up your puppy or trying to give the canine people food. Make sure people who want to play with your little dog understand that you are training your puppy, so they need to abide by the rules you've established. All playing with the puppy should be done on his level, without picking him up.

Photo Courtesy of
Jennifer Belak

Properly Greeting New People

Training your Aussiedoodle how to treat visitors could take time because of how excited the breed can be to meet new people.

The following are ways to approach introducing your puppy to a new person.

HELPFUL TIP

New Experiences in Puppyhood Are Key

Puppies have a very small window of time to get used to new experiences. Before he turns six months old, you should introduce your Aussiedoodle puppy to as many people, pets, and experiences as possible (including a trip to the groomer). Dogs that get plenty of socialization as puppies tend to be better adjusted as adults.

1. Try to have your puppy meet new people daily, if possible. This could be during walks or other activities where you get out of the house. If you can't meet new people daily, try for at least 4 times a week.

2. Invite friends and family over, and let them spend a few minutes just giving the puppy attention. If your puppy has a favorite game or activity, let people know so that they can play with the puppy. This will win the little guy over very quickly.

3. Once your puppy is old enough to learn tricks (after the first month – don't try to teach tricks in the beginning), demonstrate the tricks for visitors who are wary of your puppy. This will be really important as your puppy gets bigger because a lot of people are nervous around larger dogs (if your dog is medium sized then you likely won't have to worry so much). This helps them see that your dog is just as clownish and playful as many of the other large breeds.

4. Avoid crowds for the first few months. When your puppy is several months to a year old, though, try to go to dog-friendly events so that your pup can learn not to be uncomfortable around a large group of people.

Behavior Around Other Dogs

"Be very careful of socializing your puppy, especially around strange dogs you do not know. For one thing, if he or she has not had their complete series of vaccinations they can pick up Parvo or Distemper very easily from the ground. Once they have had their shots you can take them out but be aware of other dogs that may hurt or scare your puppy, and don't let him or her get overwhelmed by other dogs. I don't like the idea of taking a young puppy to a dog park at all. It can make or break them for socializing with other dogs."

Pam Keith
Doodles Galore

Once your puppy has had all of the vaccinations, you can start having friends and family with friendly dogs come over for a play date. Romping around the home with another dog can teach your Aussiedoodle that dogs can play in a way that people can't – if he hasn't already learned that during walks. By inviting over friends and family who have well-behaved

Photo Courtesy of
Ada Chan

and friendly dogs of all sizes, you can make socialization much easier in the early days.

When going for walks, you may want to be a little more cautious because you won't be as familiar with all of the dogs you meet. You don't want your puppy to try to meet an old dog that isn't feeling well or a dog that is not properly so- cialized because these kinds of interactions can teach your Aussiedoodle to be wary of walks. Walks should always be fun and enjoyable, so you will need to ask others who are walking their dogs if you can introduce your puppy instead of letting your puppy just run up to them. People with less sociable dogs or older dogs will let you know if their dog isn't sociable, so you can walk on, keeping your puppy on the opposite side of your body from the less friendly dog. This

Photo Courtesy of
Amy Johnson

is part of leash training too, so it is good practice to make sure to keep away from other dogs until you can confirm that the dog is safe.

Dog parks can be a fantastic place for Aussiedoodles. They get a chance to get out and play with other dogs, wearing them out without tiring you too much. You can also conduct training at a dog park when there isn't another dog there. In the beginning, go to the park when there are only a couple of dogs around so you can ensure that your Aussiedoodle does not get over stimulated. When your dog is still young, you don't want him to learn bad habits from other dogs. You do want to be able to have a bit more control, which you won't have if the park has half a dozen dogs or more roaming free. After a year or two, it will be fine to let your dog romp with many dogs, but do be more cautious in the beginning.

CHAPTER 9
Living With Other Dogs

Given their affable nature, bringing an Aussiedoodle into your home isn't likely to make a lot of waves – at least not for your puppy. The question really is how your other dog or dogs will react to having a new puppy in the home. Older dogs are less likely to be welcoming, as well as certain breeds.

The initial meeting always needs to be done outside of the home, with somewhere open, like a park, being a good place as long as there aren't a lot of other dogs around to distract the puppy during the introduction. Puppies will be easier to introduce than adult dogs, but that doesn't mean that you won't have any issues. Your new Aussiedoodle pup is likely to be excited and eager to meet your dog. It is up to you to make sure that the first encounter goes well by monitoring how your dog reacts to the puppy.

Photo Courtesy of Trista Caudill

Photo Courtesy of Gina Teague

On the plus side, having a dog already in your home can help your puppy become socialized earlier, as well as teach your puppy how things work in your home. Given how smart your puppy is likely to be, this could simplify the training process. If your current dog has any undesirable behaviors, you may want to try to work those out before your puppy arrives – you don't want your Aussiedoodle learning bad habits.

Introducing Your New Puppy

"Get another family member or friend to help you for this one: If you have another dog in the house already, walk him/her down the block, or to a park, and introduce the puppy there on neutral turf for their first meeting. Then walk home together. It's rather like the older dog invites pup home."

Sheron MW Steele, PhD
XANADU of the Rockies

Photo Courtesy of
Kennedy Hebert

Always introduce new dogs – even puppies – in a neutral place away from your home. Even if you have never had problems with your current dog, you are about to change its world. Select a park or other public area where your dog will not feel territorial. Once you know where you want to have the introduction, it's time to start planning the meeting. This gives the animals the opportunity to meet and get to know each other before entering your home together.

One of the people who should be there is the person who is in charge of the home. This helps establish the pack hierarchy. When you introduce your dog and puppy, make sure you have at least one other adult with you so there's a person to manage the other canine. If you have more than one dog, then you should have one adult per dog. This will make it easier to keep all of the dogs under control. Even the best dogs can get overly excited about meeting a puppy, and they can accidentally hurt the puppy.

Don't hold onto your puppy when the dogs meet. The puppy should have all four paws on the ground so that he doesn't feel trapped. Being on the ground means that the puppy can run if he feels threatened, and probably try to hide behind you. Stand near the puppy with your feet a little bit apart, giving your puppy a place to put distance between him and your dog.

If you are introducing multiple dogs, introduce one dog at a time to keep the puppy from being overwhelmed. Your dogs may get a little restless, but they can wait their turn. This will give the puppy a better chance to sniff each dog.

Watch for raised hackles on your dog. The puppy and each dog should have a few minutes to sniff each other, making sure that there is always slack in the leash. This helps the animals feel more relaxed since they won't feel like you are trying to restrain them. Your dog will likely either want to play or will simply ignore the puppy.

- If they want to play, just be careful that the dog doesn't accidentally hurt the puppy.
- If the dog ends up ignoring the puppy after an initial sniff, that is fine too.

If your dog's hackles are up or if your dog is clearly unhappy, keep them apart until your dog seems more comfortable.

Don't force the meeting.

The introduction could take a while, depending on individual dog personalities. The friendlier and more accepting your dog is, the easier it will be to incorporate your new puppy into the home. For some dogs a week is enough

Photo Courtesy of
Gina Teague

time to start feeling comfortable together. For other dogs, it could take a couple of months before they are fully accepting of the new puppy. Since this is a completely new dynamic in your household, your current dog may not be pleased with you bringing a little bundle of energy into his daily life. This is enough to make anyone unhappy, but especially a dog that has grown accustomed to a certain lifestyle. The older your dog is, the more likely it is that a puppy will be an unwelcome addition. Older dogs can get cranky around puppies that don't understand the rules or don't seem to know when enough is enough. The goal is to make your puppy feel welcome and safe, while letting your older dog know that your love for him is just as strong as ever.

Once home, take the dogs into the yard and remove the leashes. You will still need to have one adult per dog, including the puppy. If they seem to be all right or the dog is indifferent to the puppy, you can let your dog inside, releash the puppy, and keep the puppy on the leash as you head back in your home.

As soon as you are back inside, put the puppy in the puppy area away from all of your dogs. All of their interactions should be monitored for the first few months.

Introducing an Adult Dog

If you are considering adopting a rescue and the organization does not know how much socialization an adult Aussiedoodle has been through and can't say how well the Aussiedoodle has gotten along with other dogs, it's best not to adopt that particular adult Aussiedoodle. As a designer breed, it is very difficult to predict how they will react to other dogs when they are adults. Their past experiences will play heavily into how they react, and most of the time you simply won't have the necessary history to know how the meeting will go.

Even if the rescue group knows that the Aussiedoodle is fine with other dogs, you have to approach the introduction and first few weeks (and probably months) with caution. The new Aussiedoodle will need his own stuff in the beginning, and should be kept in a separate area when you aren't around until you know that the dogs are fairly comfortable with each other.

Plan for the introduction between your current dog and your new adult Aussie to take at least an hour. It probably won't take that long, but you must make sure that all of the dogs are comfortable during the introduction.

Follow the same steps to introduce your current dogs with your new dog as you would with a puppy.

- Start on neutral territory.
- Have one adult human per dog present at the introduction (this is even more important when introducing an adult).
- Introduce one dog at a time – don't let several dogs meet your new Aussiedoodle at one time. Having multiple dogs approaching at once in an unfamiliar environment with people the Aussiedoodle doesn't know very well – you can probably see how this can be nerve-racking for any new dog.

Unlike with a puppy, make sure to bring treats to the meeting of adult dogs. The animals will respond well to the treats, and you will have a way to quickly distract all of the dogs if they are too tense with each other.

During the introduction, watch the Aussiedoodle and your dogs to see if they raise their hackles. This is one of the first really obvious signs that a dog is uncomfortable. If either of the dogs' hackles are up, back off the introductions for a little bit. Do this by calling your current dog back first. This is also when you should start waving treats around. Avoid pulling on the leashes to separate them. You don't want to add physical tension to the situation because that could trigger a fight. Treats will work for all dogs present in the beginning, and your other dogs should be able to respond to your calling their names.

If any of the dogs are showing their teeth or growling, call your dog back and give the dogs a chance to settle down first. Use the treats and a calming voice to get them to relax. You want them all to feel comfortable during the first meeting, so you can't force the friendship. If they seem uncomfortable or wary at first, you will need to let them move at their own pace.

Establishing The New Norm

"Your Aussiedoodle is connected to you as part of your family. The best way to approach another pet is an open, friendly attitude on your part. Watch for fear or apprehension in the other pet to be sure they are okay with getting acquainted. If you approach with fear and worry, then your baby will be more likely to tense up and show anxiety."

Adrian Booher
Sunset Hill Farm

The sense of familiarity established during the first meeting doesn't mean that the dogs will have automatically bonded, and tension over that first month is relatively common. After all, you have brought a new dog into the home, which can make some dogs nervous or worried. This is why it is important to keep them separated in the home, particularly when you're away. The puppy should be in his designated area, to make it easier for him to relax and start to get familiar with the new environment. If you adopt an adult, the same thing holds true, but you will likely need to have an entire room for your new dog.

Make sure that none of your other dog's stuff ends up in the puppy's area or the place where your new Aussiedoodle spends time when you are gone. When the puppy invariably chews on everything he can reach, this will generate unnecessary tension. This is even more true if you bring home an adult and your current dog starts to feel nervous about losing his place in the pack. Before letting your puppy or new Aussiedoodle out of his designated area, make sure to do a bit of cleanup around the house and store your older dog's toys in a safe place.

Mealtime is another potential problem, so you should feed your puppy in a different location, at least in the beginning. Food tends to be the source of most dog fights. As your puppy gets older, you can start to feed him with your other dogs, but still keep them somewhat separated.

Your current dog probably isn't going to be happy about sharing you with the puppy. Schedule one-on-one time with your current dog, including longer walks, extra training, or general play. This will let your dog know that the puppy is not a replacement. You should start keeping a schedule with your dog so that you don't change the amount of time you spend together after the puppy arrives. It also means you will need to be just as firm and consistent with your puppy as you are with your dog. If you are more lenient with your puppy, this will create tension.

Photo Courtesy of Isabel DeWitt

There are a number of benefits to having a dog in the home that already knows the rules. The biggest is that your dog will reprimand your puppy for misbehavior and help him learn his place in the pack. Of course, your dog can't be the primary trainer, but it's nice to have someone helping reinforce the rules. As long as your dog is gentle, let him discipline the puppy – just make sure there isn't too much aggression or roughness to the behavior correction. Should your dog opt out of this role, that's fine. It's best to let your dog decide what kind of relationship he wants to have with the puppy.

Once your Aussiedoodle accepts your other dogs (and vice versa), he will be as protective of your dogs as he is of you. This can be wonderfully entertaining, particularly if you have bigger dogs. It is nearly certain that your Aussiedoodle is going to be the most outgoing of the bunch, and that can lead to some very interesting encounters. Being smart, your Aussiedoodle will quickly learn when to step up for your dogs and with proper socialization, that will not be often, making your trips outside enjoyable. While it is likely they will get along well, it is best to plan for the worst so that you can enjoy the fun that much more.

Biting, Fighting, And Puppy Anger Management With Multiple Puppies

You have to be firm in the early days, making sure that your puppy learns not to bite anyone (including animals) from a very early age. Adopting more than one puppy at a time is at least twice as much work. If you want to raise more than one Aussiedoodle puppy at one time, you are in for a real challenge, in part because they will learn the bad habits from each other, and are more likely to nip each other when you aren't around. They are going to want to please you and spend time with you, but they will have the same energy level, which means that their misbehaviors can feed off each other. It will take a lot more energy and work to make sure they behave appropriately.

Be prepared to lose your personal life, particularly your social life, if you have more than one puppy at a time. Taking care of those little puppies is going to be like having two full-time jobs. First, you must spend time with them both, together and separately. This means spending twice as much time with the puppies, making sure they get along well, learn at an even pace, and still get to have designated time alone with you. Each puppy will have its own strengths and weaknesses, and you need to learn what those are for each one, as well as learning how well the puppies work together. If they both behave during alone time with you, but tend to misbehave or fail to listen when they are together, you will need to adjust your approach to make sure they both understand the rules. This is a real challenge, especially if they whine when you're playing with one of them and not the other (which is very likely with Aussiedoodles).

You can always have someone else play or train with one puppy while you do the same with the other, then switch puppies. This builds bonds while letting the puppies know that they both have to listen to you and your training partner. Both puppies will also be happily occupied, so they won't be whimpering or feeling lonely while you're playing with the other puppy.

There may be some fighting between the puppies and you need to stop that immediately. Over time, you should be able to work out any aggressive behavior as long as you are consistent from the beginning. As long as they understand the rules and abide by them, your Aussiedoodles likely won't give you too much trouble.

Older Dogs And Your Aussiedoodle Puppy

"Aussiedoodles love playing with other dogs. Please make sure that the other dogs are up to date on vaccinations. Your puppy will not be totally protected until they have had their 16 week vaccination."

Mary Ann McGregor
Hearthside Country

If your dog is older, keep in mind that puppies are energetic and likely to keep trying to engage the older dog in play. This can be incredibly trying for your older pup, which is something you definitely need to keep in mind when your puppy and your dog interact. Make sure that your older canine isn't getting too tired of the puppy's antics because you don't want your puppy to learn to snap at other dogs. Be mindful of how your older dog feels and make sure the old boy is comfortable when the puppy is around, and that there is plenty of time without the puppy to pester him. Also give your older canine a lot of dedicated alone time so that he knows you still love him – this will make it easier to accept that the puppy is not a replacement, but an addition.

Once your Aussiedoodle is ready to leave the puppy area for good, you will still want to make sure that your older dog has safe places to go to be alone in case he or she just doesn't feel up to being around a spry young thing. This will reduce the likelihood that your puppy will get repeatedly scolded and therefore learn to be wary of older dogs. You definitely don't want your older dog to snap at your puppy, undoing any training you have been working on not to nip or bite.

HELPFUL TIP
Curb Herding Tendencies

Australian Shepherds were bred to herd cattle, so your Aussiedoodle may have an instinct to herd your other pets, who may not appreciate it. Do your best to curb herding tendencies in your Aussiedoodle to prevent fights with other dogs who don't want to be chased.

CHAPTER 10
Training Your Aussiedoodle Puppy

"Aussiedoodles are one of the easiest breeds to train that I've encountered in 44 years of breeding/training. They are so 'in tune' with their people that they sense nuances. This is a double edged sword if you are not a good trainer, or neglect training; as they will also train themselves to self satisfy. But, overall, a bit of training goes a 'long' way. I've had schools label my pups as 'brains wrapped in hair'."

Joyce Wallace
Pecan Place Aussiedoodles

Coming from two intelligent, hardworking dogs, odds are your Aussiedoodle is going to be very trainable, including learning tricks that go well beyond the basic commands. Of course, getting your puppy to understand the basic commands will probably be a bit of a challenge. However, once your puppy has the basics down, other tricks will come a lot more easily. Spend a few minutes checking out videos of people training their Aussiedoodles, Australian Shepherds, and Poodles. That is the potential your puppy has. Keep that potential in mind during training sessions to help keep frustration in check.

The important thing is to make training fun. That said, you still have to be firm and consistent. Any training commands that you teach during a training session have to be made to apply outside of the session too.

FUN FACT
One Smart Cookie

Australian Shepherds and Standard Poodles are two of the smartest dog breeds. That means Aussiedoodles are also very intelligent. That should make training your puppy a breeze!

Each training session is likely to leave you feeling pretty tired. Puppies simply can't focus the way adult dogs do. There are just too many distractions and things to explore as a puppy. By making sure to follow through with a few actions, you will find that your Aussiedoodle will pick up on the training much quicker.

Firm And Consistent

No matter how tired or frustrated you are, you cannot give in to the idea that something is good enough or close enough. With an Aussiedoodle, you are almost certainly dealing with a dog that is more intelligent than the average breed, and that means they are going to pick up on this attitude. From there, you are going to have a rough time because they are typically going to expect that you will give in when they make things difficult for you. With that intellect, they are going to realize if you are willing to give an inch, there is probably more you will be able to give. They are going to push those boundaries to see just how far they can go, and that will make training far less effective – if not totally unproductive. Exceptions and leniency are seen by your puppy as having some control over the situation, and that makes it much harder for him to take you seriously.

Photo Courtesy of
Christi Joyce

Be firm and consistent to keep the rules and lines clear. You must enforce the rules no matter how long a day you have had or how tired you are.

Operant Conditioning Basics

Operant conditioning is the scientific term for actions and consequences. You must provide your Aussiedoodle puppy with the right consequences for each behavior.

The best way to use operant conditioning is through positive reinforcement, particularly since Aussiedoodles are so attached to people. This type of training is more effective with working dogs and dogs that have a long history with people. They want to work with you and fulfill their tasks. Knowing that they are doing something right does a lot more to encourage their

Photo Courtesy of
Denise McCoy

behavior than knowing when they do something wrong. They will keep trying until they get it right.

There are two types of reinforcements for operant conditioning:

• Primary reinforcements
• Secondary reinforcements

You will use both during your Aussiedoodle training.

Primary Reinforcements

A primary reinforcement gives your dog something that he needs to
survive, like food or social interaction. Initially, you will rely on primary reinforcements since you don't have to teach your Aussiedoodle to enjoy them.
However, you have to keep a balance. Mealtime and playtime should never
be denied to your puppy, no matter how poorly he performs. These things
are essential to living, and are nonnegotiable. It is things like treats and extra playtime that you use to reinforce good behavior.

Err on the side of providing too much affection over too many treats.
If you rely on treats instead of attention, you are setting yourself and your
pup up for serious health problems later.

Secondary Reinforcements

Without a doubt, Pavlov's experiment with dogs is the most recogniz-
able example of secondary reinforcement. Pavlov taught test dogs to associate the ringing of a bell to mealtime. They were conditioned to associate
something with a primary reinforcement. You can see this in your home
when you use a can opener. If you have any cats or dogs, they probably
come running as soon as the can opener starts going.

Secondary reinforcements work because your Aussiedoodle will associate the trigger with something that is required. This makes your puppy
more likely to do as he is told. Dogs that are taught to sit using a treat only
will automatically react by sitting down when you have a treat in your hand.
They won't even wait for you to tell them to sit. They know that sitting means
more food, so they automatically do it once you make that association. Of
course, this is not proper training because they need to learn to sit when
you say sit, and not just when you have a treat. That is the real challenge.

Photo Courtesy of
Jean Diaz

Fortunately, it is relatively easy to train Aussiedoodle puppies with the right trigger because they are both intelligent and eager to please. While they may enjoy food, you can show them that the trigger is a word, not food.

You can also use toys and attention as a way of getting your Aussiedoodle to do the right thing. You can take the pup on an extra walk, spend a little more time playing with a favorite toy, or take some time to cuddle.

Sometimes punishment is required too, but you need to be very careful about how you do it. Trying to punish an Aussiedoodle can be tricky, but denying your Aussiedoodle attention can work very well. Simply put your puppy in a penned off area where he can see you but cannot interact with you. The little guy will whine and whimper to let you know that he wants out. Don't give in. Just ignore your puppy for as long as the pup makes noise to teach the lesson about proper behavior.

Punishments must happen right after the event. If your Aussiedoodle chews something up and you don't find out for several hours, it's too late to punish the puppy. The same is true for rewards. To reinforce behavior, the reward or punishment must be almost immediate. When you praise or punish your puppy, make sure you keep eye contact. You can also take the puppy by the scruff of the neck to ensure that you keep eye contact. You won't need to do that when you're praising your pooch because he will automatically keep eye contact. Aussiedoodles can be absolutely driven by hearing your praise.

Why Food Can Be A Bad Reinforcement Tool

All dogs are prone to overeating, just like people. The more food you give your puppy as a way to positively reinforce actions or behaviors, the more food your puppy is going to come to expect. You don't know how big your Aussiedoodle is going to be as an adult, which means that you have to remain vigilant about not overfeeding your puppy. Sure, the puppy is more than likely going to quickly burn off those calories now, but you set a dangerous precedent for later when your Aussiedoodle's metabolism slows.

Treats should only be used in the early stages when your puppy has not been conditioned to respond to secondary reinforcements. This will give you something to help your puppy learn to focus as you train the puppy to understand other incentives. It should not take too long before you can start transitioning away from treats as a reinforcement tool.

Treats are best for the beginning commands (sit, stay, and leave it). Your dog does not understand words yet, and will quickly make the connection between what you are saying and why the treat is being offered. Treats are also the best way of training certain types of behavior, such as rolling over. Your puppy will automatically follow the treat, making it easy to understand what you mean. Leave it is very difficult to teach without treats because there is no incentive to drop something if your puppy really wants the object already in his or her mouth. Treats are something that will make the puppy drop whatever is in his mouth in order to get the tasty tidbit. Once your puppy understands Leave it, you really should not use treats for training.

Small Steps To Success

Just as you don't begin with the expectation that your puppy will be housetrained in a week, you can't expect your puppy to grasp any of the initial commands within a week. Most or all of them are going to take your puppy time to comprehend what you mean, and you should not be introducing new commands until your puppy masters the current command. Additionally, your puppy must learn the daily routine. Once the schedule and environment are less new and exciting, your Aussiedoodle will have an easier time focusing during training sessions.

Basic Behavior Training

Behavioral training is different than command training, which is covered in the next chapter. Behavioral training is making sure that the behaviors you don't want in your puppy are removed before they become bad habits. Nipping and attention seeking are the biggest potential problems, so be prepared for a bit of tough love and reprimands to eliminate these behaviors. This kind of training is not restricted to just training sessions. It's something you need to constantly teach your puppy over the course of the day.

Chewing And Nipping

Chewing and nipping are behaviors you want to stop as soon as possible because it will be much harder to stop them once your puppy is an adult.

- Say no in a strong, confident voice whenever your Aussiedoodle starts chewing on anything that is not a toy or food or nips at you, another person, or another pet.
- Provide chew toys.
- Keep your Aussiedoodle in the puppy area until he no longer chews on furniture and items in reach.
- Get some puzzle toys to keep your Aussiedoodle's brain engaged.

Crate Training

Your Aussiedoodle's crate needs to be comfortable. Never treat the crate like it is a prison for your puppy. Your Aussiedoodle should never associate the crate with punishment – it is meant to be a safe haven after overstimulation or when it is time to sleep. The puppy's crate must be a safe place, so you should not associate it with punishment or negative emotions.

As mentioned in an earlier chapter, you can actually use the crate to help with housetraining. The desire not to have a dirty bed or having a safe area is going to keep your Aussiedoodle from using it as a bathroom. Having a pee pad in the puppy's area but as far from the crate as possible will help to make the point that it is to be used for bladder relief.

Puppies younger than six months old shouldn't be in the crate more than four hours at a time. They will not be able to hold their bladders that long, so you need to make sure they have a way to get out and use the restroom in an acceptable place. If you have an adult dog that is not housetrained, you will need to follow the same rules. Even though they can hold their bladders a lot longer, they haven't yet learned that they need to hold it. This is why it is up to you to make sure they get out every three to four hours to use the bathroom.

Make sure that the door is set so that it doesn't close on your dog during that initial sniff of the crate. You don't want your Aussiedoodle to get hit by the door and scare him.

1. Let your Aussiedoodle sniff the crate. You can talk to them while they do this, and you should use a positive, happy voice when you do. Associate the first experience with excitement and positive emotions so that your dog understands it is a good place. If you have a blanket form the mother, put it in the crate to help provide an extra sense of comfort.

2. Drop a couple of treats into the crate if your canine seems resistant to enter it. Do NOT force your puppy into the crate. If your dog doesn't want to go all the way into this strange little space, that is perfectly fine. It has to be their decision to enter so that it isn't a negative experience.

3. Feed your dog in the crate for a week or two. This will help create some very positive emotions with the crate, as well as helping you to keep the food away from other dogs if you have them.

   a. If your dog appears comfortable with the crate, put the food all the way at the back.

   b. If not, place the food bowl in the front, then move it further back in the crate over time.

4. Start closing the door once your dog appears to be eating comfortably in the crate. When the food is gone, open the crate immediately.

5. Leave the door closed for longer periods of time after eating. If your pup begins to whine, you have left your Aussiedoodle in the crate for too long.

6. Crate your dog for longer periods of time once your dog shows no signs of discomfort in the crate when eating. You can start to train them to go

to the crate by simply saying "crate" or "bed," then praise your dog to let him know that he has done a great job.

Repeat this for several weeks until your dog feels comfortable. Doing this several times each day can help your dog to learn that everything is all right and the crate is not a punishment. Initially, you will be doing this while you are still at home or when you go out to get the mail. As soon as your puppy can make it for half an hour without whining and you out of the room, you can start leaving your pup alone while you are gone, keeping the time short (not more than an hour) in the beginning.

Once your dog understands not to tear up your home, the crate training is complete.

Monitoring Aggression

Aggression isn't typically a problem, but you can never be entirely certain with a designer breed. As loving as most Aussiedoodles are, there isn't enough data or history to guarantee that there won't be at least a little aggression.

One of the best ways to reduce potential aggression is to make sure your dog gets adequate exercise and playtime. Chapter 13 goes into detail about exercising your Aussiedoodle. By tiring your pup out, you drastically reduce any chance that your puppy is going to be agitated because of too much pent-up energy. Training is another great way to help you get a better understanding of your puppy's temperament and how much energy the little guy has. The mental stimulation of training also acts as a way to keep your puppy from getting bored, making it much less likely that your puppy will act out with aggression.

The Constant Hunt For Attention

More likely than aggression, your Aussiedoodle is probably going to look for ways to get your attention. Like toddlers and young kids, this could mean that your Aussiedoodle turns to any means of getting your attention, even if that attention is negative. This can be in different ways of acting out, like destroying something or barking. This is when avoiding punishment is difficult, but over time you will learn to deal with it.

Since what they really want is your attention, the best way to train them that they cannot demand it is by ignoring them when they act out. If they are barking, don't acknowledge them. Once they stop barking, count to 5, then praise them for the quiet. If they are destroying items that they aren't meant to destroy, remove the items that you don't want them to harm.

Ignoring your dog is what works best to train out the attention-seeking behavior. As difficult as that may be, it is necessary to keep your puppy from learning how to push your buttons. After all, you do not want those behaviors to escalate as an adult because they will be able to do a lot more damage and their voices will be a lot louder.

What Classes And Trainers Offer Aussiedoodle Parents

Classes can be a great way to help socialize your dog when he is young. If you don't have much experience training a dog, classes have a lot to offer you by helping you see how to train and what kinds of methods work for different dogs.

Odds are, your dog will be the only Aussiedoodle in the class, and many trainers are not going to have experience with such a new breed. However, they probably have worked with other Poodle mixes, and that knowledge is going to be largely applicable. They basically train you in how to train your dog.

If you have experience in training dogs, classes and individual trainers really are not necessary with the Aussiedoodle. They are inclined to listen to a person they respect and who has taken a firm and consistent approach with them. Unless you want to give them another way to socialize, you should be just fine training them in the same way you have trained other dogs (as long as your previous training was successful).

If your Aussiedoodle starts to exhibit behavior issues and you aren't sure how to handle it, then you can hire a professional trainer for a few one-on-one sessions. Given that most trainers probably have not trained an Aussiedoodle before, you may want to look for someone who has experience with Australian Shepherds or Poodle mixes. They will have a better idea of what could be triggering the undesirable behavior, and how best to counter it.

Photo Courtesy of Shelby Robinson

CHAPTER 11
Basic Commands

"Aussiedoodles are very easy to train with consistent expectations. In a large family where each family member has a different way of requesting a command, a puppy might hesitate more, but even then, will quickly learn each cue and each request. Both the Poodle and the Aussie were bred to respond to commands, be eager to please, and show high intelligence."

Adrian Booher
Sunset Hill Farm

Photo Courtesy of Angie Shade

With more than a decade of potential training ahead of you, there are so many kinds of fun tricks that your dog will be more than happy to learn. Commands like roll over, high five, and play dead may take a little more time to teach, but your dog can learn them and will love to show off in front of everyone. Fetch will probably be surprisingly easy for your Aussiedoodle to learn, so if you like to play Frisbee or ball, your dog will be absolutely delighted to play with you.

All of these are things that you may very well be able to train your dog to do later, but first you and your puppy have to get through the first few commands. That will be a bit trickier because you are both going to be learning.

Picking The Right Reward

The right reward for an Aussiedoodle will ultimately be love and affection. However, in the beginning, you are probably going to need treats, at least until your puppy understands that certain words mean that the puppy should be doing certain actions. Treats are the easiest way of keying a puppy into the idea that performing tricks is a good behavior.

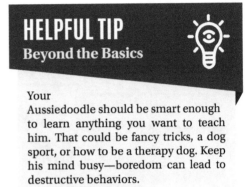

HELPFUL TIP
Beyond the Basics

Your Aussiedoodle should be smart enough to learn anything you want to teach him. That could be fancy tricks, a dog sport, or how to be a therapy dog. Keep his mind busy—boredom can lead to destructive behaviors.

Soon though, you will need to switch to something that is a secondary reinforcer. Praise, additional playtime, and extra petting are all fantastic rewards for Aussiedoodles since they care about how you feel and how you react to them. Plopping down to watch a movie and letting your puppy sit with you is a great reward after an intense training session. Not only did your puppy learn, but you both now get to relax together.

Basic Commands

There are five basic commands that all dogs should know. These commands are the basis for a happy and enjoyable relationship with your dog. By the time your puppy learns all five of the commands, it will be more obvious what the correlation between words you say and the expected actions are. This will clue the dog in to understanding new words in terms of expectation. That will make it much easier to train him on the more complex concepts.

Train your puppy to do the commands in the order they appear in this chapter. Sit is a basic command, and something all dogs already naturally do. Since dogs tend to sit often, it is the easiest one to teach. Teaching leave it is much more difficult, and it usually requires that the puppy fight an instinct or desire. Consider how much you give in to something you want to do when you know you shouldn't – that's pretty much what you are facing, but with a puppy. Quiet can be another difficult command as dogs (particularly puppies) tend to bark as a natural reaction to something. These two commands will take longer to teach, so you want to have the necessary tools already in place to increase your odds of success.

Photo Courtesy of
Jen Smith

Here are some basic guidelines to follow during training.

- Include everyone in the home in the Aussiedoodle training. The puppy must learn to listen to everyone in the household, and not just one or two people. A set training schedule may only involve a couple people in the beginning, especially if you have children. There should always be an adult present for training, but including one child during training will help reinforce the idea that the puppy listens to everyone in the house. It is also a good way for the parent to monitor the child's interaction so that everyone plays in a way that is safe and follows the rules.

- To get started, select an area where you and your puppy have no distractions, including noise. Leave your phone and other devices out of range so that you keep your attention on the puppy.

- Stay happy and excited about the training. Your puppy will pick up on your enthusiasm, and will focus better because of it.

- Be consistent and firm as you teach.

- Bring a special treat to the first few training sessions, such as chicken or small treats.

Sit

Start to teach sit when your puppy is around eight weeks old. Once you settle into your quiet training location with a special treat, begin the training.

1. Hold out the treat.

2. Move the treat over your puppy's head. This will make the puppy move back.

3. Say sit as the puppy's haunches touch the floor.

Having a second person around to demonstrate this with your puppy will be helpful as they can sit to show what you mean.

Wait until your puppy starts to sit down and say sit as he or she sits. If your puppy finishes sitting down, start to give praise. Naturally, this will make your puppy incredibly excited and wiggly, so it may take a bit of time before he or she will want to sit again. When the time comes and the puppy starts to sit again, repeat the process.

It's going to take more than a couple of sessions for the puppy to fully connect your words with the actions. Commands are something completely new to your little companion. Once your puppy has demonstrated a mastery over sit, it is time to start teaching down.

Photo Courtesy of Emma Caviness

Down

Repeat the same process to teach this command as you did for sit.

1. Tell your dog to sit.

2. Hold out the treat.

3. Lower the treat to the floor with your dog sniffing at it. Allow for your pup to lick the treat, but if your dog stands up, start over.

4. Say down as the puppy's elbows touch the floor, then give praise while letting your puppy each the treat.

Wait until the puppy starts to lie down, then say the word. If the Aussiedoodle finishes the action, offer your chosen reward.

It will probably take a little less time to teach this command.

Wait until your puppy has mastered down before moving on to stay.

Stay

This command is going to be more difficult since it isn't something that your puppy does naturally. Be prepared for it to take a bit longer to train on this command. It is also important that your dog has mastered and will consistently sit and lie down on command before you start to teach stay. Stay can keep your puppy from running across a street or from running at someone who is nervous or scared of dogs.

Tell your puppy to either sit or stay. As you do this, place your hand in front of the puppy's face. Wait until the puppy stops trying to lick your hand before you begin again.

When the puppy settles down, take a step away from the Aussiedoodle. If your puppy is not moving, say stay and give a treat and some praise for staying.

Giving the reward to your puppy indicates that the command is over, but you also need to indicate that the command is complete. The puppy has to learn to stay until you say it is okay to leave the spot. Once you give the okay to move, do not give treats. Come should not be used as the okay word as it is a command used for something else.

Repeat these steps, taking more steps further from the puppy after a successful command.

Once your puppy understands stay when you move away, start training to stay even if you are not moving. Extend the amount of time required for

the puppy to stay in one spot so that he understands that stay ends with the okay command.

When you feel that your puppy has stay mastered, start to train the puppy to come.

Come

This is a command you can't teach until the puppy has learned the previous commands. Before you start, decide if you want to use come or come here for the command. You will need to be consistent in the words you use.

This command is important for the same reason as the previous one. If you are around people who are nervous around dogs, or encounter a wild animal or other distraction, this command can snap your puppy's attention back to you.

Leash the puppy.

Tell the puppy to stay. Move away from the puppy.

Say the command you will use for come and give a gentle tug on the leash toward you. Repeat these steps, building a larger distance between you and the puppy. Once the puppy seems to get it, remove the leash and start at a close distance. If your puppy doesn't seem to understand the command, give some visual clues about what you want. For example, you can pat your leg or snap your fingers. As soon as your puppy comes running over to you, offer a reward.

Leave It

This is going to be one of the most difficult commands you will teach your puppy because it goes against both your puppy's instincts and interests. Your puppy wants to keep whatever he has, so you are going to have to offer something better. It is essential to teach the command early though, as your Aussiedoodle is going to be very destructive in the early days. You want to get the trigger in place to convince the puppy to drop things. Furthermore this command could save your pooch's life. He is likely to lunge at things that look like food when you are out for a walk. This command gets him to drop any potentially hazardous meal.

You will need two different types of treats for this command. Since this is a more advanced basic command, your puppy will probably already be bored with one type of treat, or at least will be less enthusiastic about it. This will be your first treat. The newer, more interesting treat will be the reward treat.

1. Put one of each treat in each hand. If you want to use a clicker too, put it with the exciting treat.

2. Hide the less exciting treat, then hold it out to your puppy to let the little guy sniff your hand.

3. Say Leave it. Your puppy will keep sniffing, so you will need to wait until the sniffing stops (even if the treat is not exciting, it is still food).

4. When your puppy stops sniffing your hand, tell him or her good and hand over the exciting treat.

5. Repeat this immediately after your puppy finishes the exciting treat.

When your puppy stops sniffing as soon as you say Leave it, you can graduate to the next phase.

1. Put the puppy's leash on.

2. Toss the less exciting treat out of reach.

3. Say Leave it and wait for the puppy to stop trying to get to the treat or trying to sniff in that direction.

4. When the puppy stops, tell him or her good and hand over the exciting treat.

You will need to keep reinforcing this command for months after it is learned because it is not a natural reaction. You can start to use your puppy's favorite toy in place of the less exciting treat. As the Aussiedoodle drops the toy, say Leave it, and hand over the treat when the puppy shows that it will not go after the toy.

This is going to be one of those rare times when you must use a treat because your puppy needs something better to convince him or her to drop the toy. For now, your puppy needs that incentive, something more tempting than what he or she already has before your puppy can learn the command.

Quiet

Aussiedoodles aren't considered excessive barkers, but there is no guarantee that yours won't be vocal. Initially, you can use treats sparingly to reinforce quiet if your pup enjoys making noise. If your puppy barks with no obvious reason, tell the puppy to be quiet and place a treat nearby. It is almost guaranteed that the dog will fall silent to sniff the treat, in which case, say good dog or good quiet. It will not take too long for your puppy to understand that quiet means no barking.

Where To Go From Here

"Aussiedoodles are known as the 'Einstein's' of the Doodle world because they are extremely smart! Aussiedoodles thrive on being trained and taught new tricks. All it takes is consistency on the owner's part."

Brey Sanchez
Marley's Doodles

This chapter provides the five essential commands that all dogs should learn. However, with any intelligent breed like the Aussiedoodle, there is a limitless number of commands for you to keep the training going for the rest of your dog's life. It is the perfect way to exercise your dog's mind while giving him lots of attention. He'll love the time with you, and you'll have a much stronger bond. Not only that, but you can train your dog to do some pretty impressive tricks for when people come to visit. There was a good reason why Poodles were one of the most popular dogs in circuses, and that desire for attention is likely to be a part of your dog's personality.

You do need to keep it toned back in the beginning though. You are still training a puppy after all, so his skills and abilities are still limited. Make sure that the tricks that you teach your Aussiedoodle are not too stressful for the puppy. As your puppy grows, you can start teaching tricks that highlight his agility. Fetch and other interactive tricks are ideal and fun.

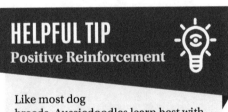

HELPFUL TIP
Positive Reinforcement

If someone in your family suffers from an illness, including mental disorders like depression or autism, Aussiedoodles can be taught to help. Poodles are a part of the support dog community, so there is definitely an ability to help when people when they need it. An Aussiedoodle will need special training, so you will need to find a professional to help train your dog (it is not something you can do on your own because it is a complicated process). Still, it is an option should someone in your family need the additional canine support.

Like most dog breeds, Aussiedoodles learn best with positive reinforcement training. That means you reward good behaviors and ignore bad behaviors. Studies are now showing that punishing dogs or using dominance-based training types is less effective than positive reinforcement.

CHAPTER 12
Nutrition

"Since the Poodle and the Aussie are different in their energy consumption, each of the puppies will be a blend of the two. There are some tendencies in both Poodles and Aussies that can manifest. Your vet is the best guide as to the nutritional needs of your specific dog."

Adrian Booher
Sunset Hill Farm

Photo Courtesy of Ariel Childers

Neither Aussiedoodle parent makes the top 10 list of breeds that are most likely to become obese, but that doesn't mean that doesn't mean that it isn't a problem for those breeds. As working dogs, they have a tendency to each all available food. Just like you have to watch what you eat, you need to be careful about what you feed your Aussiedoodle.

Proper nutrition begins in puppyhood. That fast metabolism doesn't mean you can be careless about what your puppy eats. Not only do you have to be careful not to give your dog food from the "do not feed" list, but you must avoid giving him food that is high in calories. As your pup gets older, this can become a serious issue. Ensuring your cute Aussiedoodle pup gets the right nutritional balance is what will ensure that he grows into a strong, healthy dog.

Canine Nutrition

The dietary needs of a dog are significantly different than a human's needs. People are more omnivorous than dogs, meaning they require a wider range of nutrients to be healthy. Canines are largely carnivorous, and protein is a significant dietary requirement. However, they need more than just protein to be healthy.

Neither of the parent breeds of the Aussiedoodle have any unique dietary needs. The following table provides the primary nutritional requirements for dogs.

Nutrient	Sources	Puppy	Adult
Protein	Meat, eggs, soybeans, corn, wheat, peanut butter	22.0% of diet	18.0% of diet
Fats	Fish oil, flaxseed oil, canola oil, pork fat, poultry fat, safflower oil, sunflower oil, soybean oil	8.0 to 15.0% of diet	5.0 to 15.0% of diet
Calcium	Dairy, animal organ tissue, meats, legumes (typically beans)	1.0% of diet	0.6% of diet
Phosphorus	Meat and pet supplements	0.8% of diet	0.5% of diet
Sodium	Meat, eggs	0.3% of diet	0.06% of diet

Source: PetMD

The following are the remaining nutrients required, all of them less than 1% of diet of the puppy or adult diet:

- Arginine
- Histidine
- Isoleucine
- Leucine
- Lysine
- Methionine + cystine
- Phenylalanine + tyrosine
- Threonine
- Tryptophan
- Valine
- Chloride

Dogs do not have a high sodium requirement. Since so many human foods contain preservatives and salt, it is best to avoid giving your dog any human foods with a lot of sodium.

Photo Courtesy of
Ruby Hunter

Water is also absolutely essential to keeping your dog healthy. There should always be water in your dog's water bowl, so make a habit of checking it several times a day so that your dog does not get dehydrated.

Proteins And Amino Acids

As carnivores, protein is one of the most important nutrients in a healthy dog's diet (though they could not eat meat nearly as exclusively as their close wolf relatives; their diets and needs have changed significantly as a companion to humans). Proteins contain the necessary amino acids for your dog to produce glucose, which is essential for giving your dog energy.

A lack of protein in your dog's diet will result in him being more lethargic, his coat may start to look duller, and he is likely to lose weight. If your dog gets too much protein, your dog's body will store the excess protein as fat, meaning he will gain weight.

Meat is typically the best source of protein, and it is recommended since a dog's dietary needs are significantly different from a human's needs. However, it is possible for a dog to have a vegetarian diet as long as you ensure that your dog gets the necessary protein through other sources, and you will need to include supplemental vitamin D in their food. If you plan to feed your dog a vegetarian diet, you need to talk to your vet before you convert your dog to this diet. It is incredibly difficult to ensure that a carnivore gets adequate protein with a vegetarian diet, especially puppies, so you will need to dedicate a lot of time to research and discussion with nutrition experts to ensure that your dog is getting the necessary proteins for his needs.

Fat And Fatty Acids

Most of the fats that your dog needs also comes from meat, though seed oils can provide a lot of the necessary healthy fats too, with peanut butter being one of the most common sources. Fats are broken down into fatty acids, which your dog needs for fat-soluble vitamins that help with regular cell functions. Perhaps the most obvious benefit of fats and fatty acids in in your dog's coat, which will be healthier if your dog is getting adequate fats in his diet.

There are a number of potential health issues if your dog does not get adequate fats in his daily diet.

- His coat will likely look less healthy.
- His skin may be dry and itchy.
- His immune system could be compromised, making it easier for your dog to get sick.

- He may have more non-communicable health issues, such as an increased risk of heart disease.

The primary concern if your dog gets too much fat is that your dog will gain weight and become obese. He may also suffer from the same non-communicable health issues, like heart problems. For breeds that are predisposed to heart problems, you need to be particularly careful to ensure your dog gets the right amount of fats in his diet.

Carbohydrates and Cooked Foods

Dogs have been living with humans for millennia, so their dietary needs have evolved like our own. They are able to eat foods with carbohydrates to supplement the energy typically provided by proteins and fats. The complex carbohydrates in grains (such as barley, corn, rice, and wheat) are more difficult for a dog to digest. If you cook up grains prior to feeding them to your dog, it will be easier for your dog to digest them. This is something to keep in mind when considering what type of food you will feed your dog as you want to get a kibble (dry dog food) that uses meat instead of grains; while your dog can digest food with grains, he won't get as much of the nutritional value as he would from food that has real meat.

Why A Healthy Diet Is Important

Just because your Aussiedoodle is active doesn't mean that he is burning all of the calories he takes in, especially if you have an open treat policy. Just as you should not be eating all day, your puppy shouldn't be either. Yes, they do need to eat a lot, but that doesn't mean anything goes. If you have a very busy schedule, it will be entirely too easy to have substantial lapses in activity levels while you are home. Your Aussiedoodle isn't going to understand your schedule changes, just the fact that there is usually a certain amount of food going into his mouth, regardless of his activity level. This means he is likely to gain weight when you keep the calories the same while reducing the activities.

You need to be aware of roughly how many calories your dog eats a day, including treats. Be aware of your dog's weight so you can see when he is putting on pounds. This will key you in to when you should adjust how much food the Aussiedoodle eats a day, or change the food to something with more nutritional value but fewer calories.

Always talk with your vet if you have concerns about your Aussiedoodle's weight.

Different stages of a dog's life have different nutritional needs.

Puppy Food

Dog food manufacturers produce a completely different type of food for puppies for a very good reason – their nutritional needs are much different than their adult counterparts. During roughly the first 12 months, their bodies are growing. To be healthy, they need more calories and have different nutritional needs to promote that growth.

There are also different types of puppy chow for different sized dogs. If your Aussiedoodle has a parent that is a Miniature Poodle, you will need a different type of puppy food than if the parent is a Standard Poodle. The body of a small dog breed does not grow very much from puppy to adulthood. Rapid growth to reach their adult size is not going to hurt their bodies since there isn't too much of a difference between the two stages.

Larger dog breeds do grow a lot between the time they are young puppies and adulthood. To reduce the strain of this growth on their bodies, large dog breeds need to grow at a more even rate. Larger breeds are already prone to different types of orthopedic ailments, like hip dysplasia, and part of this is because of how much their bodies change during the first couple of years. Rapid growth as a puppy can exacerbate orthopedic ailments. Nutrition that encourages a more evenly paced growth is typically marked as being for large breed puppies. Dog food for large puppy dog breeds has less fat, calcium, and phosphorous, with particularly care given to the balance of phosphorous and calcium to keep the growth at a steady instead of rapid rate. They will still reach their full size, but their bodies will grow at a more steady rate.

Adult Dog Food

There is no set period of when you should switch from giving your dog puppy food to giving him adult food. The primary difference between the two is that puppy food is higher in calories and nutrients that promote growth. Dog food producers reduce these nutrients in food made for adult dogs as they no longer need to sustain growth. As a general rule, when a dog reaches about 90% of his predicted adult size, you should switch to adult dog food.

As adults, dogs have pretty much the same nutritional needs, but the size of your dog is key in determining how much to feed him. The following table is a general recommendation on how much to feed your adult Aussiedoodle a day. Initially, you may want to focus on the calories as you try to find the right balance for your dog.

Photo Courtesy of Trista Caudill

Dog Size	Cups	Calories
25 to 40 lbs.	1.5 to 2.0	576 and 969
40 to 50 lbs.	2.25 to 2.5	969 and 1,145
50 to 60 lbs.	2.5 to 3.0	1,145 and 1,31
60 to 75 lbs.	3 to 3.5	1,313 and 1,600

This scale is for a dog's ideal weight range. If your dog is overweight or obese, you need to listen to your vet about how much you should be feeding your dog a day.

Also keep mind that these recommendations are per day, and not per meal. It will be much easier to provide your dog a single meal with the right measurement than if you feed your dog multiple meals. Then again, your dog probably won't like it very much when you eat several meals compared to his one meal. If you want to feed your dog when you eat, make sure that you carefully measure out how much food you give your dog with each meal so that you do not exceed the daily recommendation. For example, if you feed your 55 lb. Aussiedoodle breakfast and dinner, you can give him 1.5 cups of food in the morning, then 1 to 1.5 cups in the evening. This will keep your dog's food intake to 2.5 to 3.0 cups each day.

If you plan to add wet food, you will need to pay attention to the total calorie intake and adjust how much you feed your dog between the kibble and wet food. In other words, you may be giving your dog less than the recommended scoops of kibble because you are adding wet food, which increases your dog's caloric intake.

The same is true if you give your dog a lot of treats over the course of the day. You should reduce how much food you give your dog at mealtime based on how many treats you give him during the day.

If you plan to feed your dog homemade food, you will need to learn more about nutrition, and you will need to pay attention to the calories, and not the cup measurements.

Senior Dog Food

Like older people, senior dogs aren't capable of being nearly as active as they were in their younger days. The size of your dog will determine when you need to make the change from regular dog food to senior food.

- Small dogs are usually considered to be seniors by the time they are 9 years old, so you should make the change from adult dog food to senior dog food by the time your small Aussiedoodle turns 9.

- Larger dogs are considered to be seniors around 7.5 to 8 years old, so you should switch to senior dog food by the time your dog turns 8.

These are just rough guidelines though. If you notice your dog slowing down or you notice that your dog isn't able to take those longer walks because of joint pain or stamina, that is a good sign that your dog's body is probably slowing down too. Switching to senior dog food is really something that should be done on an individual basis. Consult with your vet when you think it is time to change the type of food you give your dog.

The primary difference between adult and senior dog food is that senior dog food has less fat and more antioxidants to help fight weight gain. Senior dogs also need more protein, which will probably make your dog happy because that usually means more meat and meat flavors. Protein helps to maintain your dog's aging muscles. He should be eating less phosphorous during his golden years.

Senior dog food is made so that it has the right calories for the reduced activity, so you shouldn't need to adjust how much food you give your dog, unless you notice that your dog is putting on weight. Consult your vet before you adjust the amount of food though, particularly if you notice that your dog is putting on weight. It could be a sign of another older dog ailment.

Photo Courtesy of
Jean Diaz

Food Allergies

Whenever you start your dog on a new type of dog food (even if it is the same brand that your dog is accustomed to, but a different flavor), you need to monitor your dog for signs of food allergies. Food allergies are not common in either parent breed, but that doesn't mean your Aussiedoodle won't have an allergic reaction to new foods.

Food allergies in dogs tend to manifest themselves as hot spots, which are similar to rashes in humans. Your dog may start scratching at specific spots on his body, and will likely chew on this location of his body if he can reach it. His fur could start falling out around the spot.

Some dogs don't have a single hot spot, but the allergy shows on their entire coat. If your Aussiedoodle seems to be shedding more fur than normal, you should take your dog to the vet to have him checked for food allergies.

Since the symptoms of food allergies and some nutritional deficiencies are similar (particularly a lack of fats in a dog's diet), you should visit your vet if you notice any problems with your dog's coat or skin.

Commercial Food

Make sure that you are buying the best dog food that you can afford. Take the time to research each of your options, particularly the nutritional value of the food, and make this an annual task. You want to make sure that the food you are giving your dog is quality food. Always account for your dog's size, energy levels, and age. Your puppy may not need puppy food as long as other breeds (or even other Aussiedoodles), and dog food for seniors may not be the best option for your senior Aussiedoodle.

Barkspace provides several great articles about which commercial dog foods are good for Aussiedoodles. Since new foods frequently come on the market, you will likely want to check back with them to see if there are newer, better foods available once a year or every other year. Since you have to be careful of your Aussiedoodle's weight, it is well worth verifying that you are giving him one of the best foods for his needs.

If you aren't sure about which food is the best one, talk with the breeder about what foods they recommend. You can ask your vet, though odds are most of them have not worked with many Aussiedoodles and haven't formed an opinion yet. This is one of the times where knowing what the breeders use will help keep your Aussiedoodle healthy as they are the real experts on the breed.

Some dogs may be picky, and they can certainly get tired of having the same food repeatedly. Just as you switch up your meals, you can change what your Aussiedoodle eats. While you aren't going to want to frequently change the brand of food (or not often), you can get foods that have different flavors. You can also change the taste by adding a bit of wet (canned) food. This is an easy change to make, giving your dog a different canned food (usually just about ¼ to 1/3 of the can for a meal, depending on your dog's size) with each meal.

For more details on commercial options, check out Dog Food Advisor. They provide reviews on the different brands, as well as providing information on recalls and contamination issues.

Pros And Cons Of Dry Dog Food

Also called kibble, dry dog food often comes in bags, and it is what the vast majority of people feed their dogs. Although large bags of food can be costly, they can last for weeks to a month, depending on the size of your dog and the bag you purchase.

The following are the primary pros of getting dry dog food:

- Convenience
- Variety
- Availability
- Affordability
- Maker follows nutritional recommendations (not all of them follow this, so do your brand research before you buy)
- Specially formulated for different canine life stages
- Can be used for training
- Easy to store

The following are the primary cons of getting dry dog food:

- Requires research to ensure you don't buy what is a doggie junk food equivalent
- Packaging is not always honest
- Recalls for food contamination
- Loose American Feed Control Officials and US Food and Drug Administration regulations
- Low quality food may have questionable ingredients

The convenience and ease on your budget means that you are almost certainly going to buy kibble for your dog. This is perfectly fine, and most dogs will be more than happy to eat kibble. Do know what brand you are currently feeding your dog, and pay attention to kibble recalls to ensure you stop feeding your dog that particular food if dog food producers find a problem with the food.

Pros And Cons Of Wet Dog Food

Most dogs prefer wet dog food to kibble, but it is also more expensive. They do come in larger packs though that can be very easy to store.

The following are the primary pros of wet dog food.

- It helps keep dogs hydrated.
- They have a richer scent and flavor.
- It is easier to eat for dogs with dental problems (particularly missing teeth) or if a dog has been ill.
- It is convenient and easy to serve (though you still need a dog bowl).
- Unopened, it can last between 1 and 3 years.
- It is balanced based on current pet nutrition recommendations.

The following are the primary cons of getting dry dog food.

- The dog bowls should be washed after every meal.
- It can soften their bowel movements.
- It can be messier than kibble.
- Once opened, it has a very short shelf life, and should be covered and refrigerated.
- It is more expensive than dry dog food, and comes in small quantities.
- Packaging is not always honest.
- Recalls for food contamination.
- Loose American Feed Control Officials and US Food and Drug Administration regulations.

Like dry dog food, wet dog food is convenient, and picky dogs are much more likely to eat it than kibble. When your dog gets sick, it is best to use wet dog food to ensure that he is eating so that he gets the necessary nutrition he needs each day. It may be a bit harder to switch back to kibble once he is healthy, but you can always continue to add a little wet food to make each meal more appetizing to your dog.

Preparing Your Dog's Food Naturally At Home

Photo Courtesy of
Jaime Matkowsky

If you regularly make your own food (from scratch, not with a microwave or boxed meal), it really doesn't take that much more time to provide an equally healthy meal for your companion.

Keeping in mind the foods that your Aussiedoodle absolutely should not eat, you can mix some of the food you make for yourself in your Aussiedoodle's meal. Just make sure to add a bit more of what your Aussiedoodle needs to the puppy food bowl. Although you and your Aussiedoodle have distinctly different dietary needs, you can tailor your foods to include nutrients that your dog needs. Read through Chapter 4 to make sure that you never give your Aussiedoodle food that could be harmful or deadly to a dog.

Do not feed your Aussiedoodle from your plate. Split the food, placing your dog's meal into a bowl so that your canine understands that your food is just for you. The best home-cooked meals should be planned in advance so that your Aussiedoodle is getting the right nutritional balance.

Typically, 50% of your dog's food should be animal protein (fish, poultry, and organ meats). About 25% should be full of complex carbohydrates. The remaining 25% should be from fruits and vegetables, particularly foods like pumpkin, apples, bananas, and green beans. These provide additional flavor that your Aussiedoodle will probably love while making the little pup feel full faster so that the chance of overeating is reduced.

The following are a couple of sites you can use to make meals for canines (the sites are not Aussiedoodle specific, so if you have more than one dog, these meals can be made for all of your furry canine friends):

- K9 of Mine

- Dogsaholic

Weight Management

One thing that working dogs expect is a schedule – and they expect that food will also be provided on a set schedule, no matter what else is thrown off schedule. As far as your Aussiedoodle is concerned, the day is based on mealtimes and training sessions, with meals being more important, if less fun. Your dog will remind you that you are forgetting something important if you feed him later than usual. If treats and snacks are something you establish as normal early on, your dog is going to believe that treats are also a part of the routine and will expect them.

Establishing a healthy balance between diet and exercise shouldn't be too difficult with an Aussiedoodle, as long as you pay attention to how much food you give your dog compared to how much exercise he gets. Get used to exercising and playing as a reward system.

Weighing your Aussiedoodle will be helpful to ensure your pooch is staying at a healthy weight. If your Aussiedoodle is small, you can do this at home with your own personal scale.

1. Step on the scale and see how much you weigh.

2. Write it down – being honest.

3. Pick up your pup and step on the scale.

4. Write the new number down.

5. Subtract how much you weigh alone from what you and your dog weigh together.

The difference is your dog's weight.

If your dog is on the larger side, the above steps aren't a good idea as picking up the dog could hurt you, your dog, or both of you. Many vets allow you to weigh your pet for free. Stopping by every few months should be sufficient for the first couple of years, then one or twice a year after your dog is an adult. If you see that your dog is gaining weight, find out what your vet recommends. Usually, they recommend reducing how much food you give your dog during the regular meals. While you should do this, it is likely that the extra food from treats and table scraps are the real reason why your dog is gaining weight. Take the time to understand what your Aussiedoodle is eating to keep his weight healthy.

CHAPTER 13
Exercising – Great Exercise Partners

"Aussiedoodles don't need a huge amount of physical exercise. They can run all day with kids, or hikers, but, if you are a homebody and don't get out much they are generally very satisfied with about an hour a day and lots of mental stimulation. Give your Aussiedoodle a mental task and they are happy campers."

Joyce Wallace
Pecan Place Aussiedoodles

HELPFUL TIP
Dog Sports

Since Aussiedoodles are very intelligent and have a ton of energy, they are great candidates to participate in dog sports like agility, flyball, or dock diving. Your dog will love the physical and mental stimulation, and you'll love bonding with your dog when you participate in a sport together.

Aussiedoodles are high energy and, though not working dogs, have a lot of the same needs as breeds with working backgrounds. You'll need to scale your exercise to fit the size of your dog – a 40 lb. dog will get more out of an hour-long walk or jog than a 75 lb. dog. Your dog should get at least an hour's worth of exercise a day, though an hour and a half should be the norm for most Aussiedoodles. Given their intelligence and the risk of them getting bored, you want to keep your Aussiedoodle either happily occupied or tired. This is much easier if you exercise several times a day in half-hour increments. On days when the weather makes it difficult, you can fall back on training to expend some of that energy.

Photo Courtesy of Cassandra Collins

Photo Courtesy of Ariel Childers

Exercise – High Energy With A Love For Working

Bringing an Aussiedoodle into your home means you are agreeing to daily exercise, even when he is still a puppy. Dogs don't want to misbehave, but if they are bored, mischief is inevitable.

While the Aussiedoodle isn't a work dog, that doesn't mean that you can't put your pal to work. When you go out for a walk, put on a body harness with things like water bottles and a Frisbee or two. Not only will the extra weight use up a little bit of energy, but your dog will love the fact that you are giving him that much more attention.

Since weight problems are directly related to a lack of exercise, if your dog is gaining weight, that could be a sign that he isn't getting enough time moving. Fortunately, it's easy; you have a lot of options for how to make sure your dog gets enough of a workout, including swimming.

A Fantastic Jogging Or Swimming Companion

"Include your dog in as many of your activities as possible: family fun, cross country skiing, swimming, hiking, pet-friendly shopping, and dog parks. Also, agility training is so much fun and great exercise. Set up an agility course in the backyard."

Sheron MW Steele, PhD
XANADU of the Rockies

If you are looking for a great jogging companion, not many breeds are as perfect as the Aussiedoodle. However, you can't start jogging with your Aussiedoodle during the first year or two. Several considerations have to be met first.

- It's best not to try to jog with your Aussiedoodle until you know that your dog understands the heel command.
- Your Aussiedoodle isn't wearing extra padding and protection on his or her feet, so as often as you can, jog on softer ground, such as dirt paths.
- Don't go for long runs in the beginning. Your Aussiedoodle needs to build up stamina and understanding of the activity.

Photo Courtesy of Jen Smith

Aussiedoodles are fabulous swimmers. On days when you go to the lake, the beach, or any other body of water, you can take your dog and have a great time. Swimming is a far more tiring activity than walking or jogging. Of course, there is more cleanup afterward, so don't forget to take a couple of towels to dry off your Aussiedoodle. You may also want to have your Aussiedoodle's coat cut before a swim to reduce how much water your pup absorbs.

Playtime!

Just because there is inclement weather doesn't mean that your dog's energy levels will be any lower, so you'll need to plan to keep your dog's exercise schedule from inside the house. Of course, if you can put your dog out to play in the snow in a backyard, that would be fantastic as he can tire himself out in his excitement at playing in the snow. For rain and heat, you are going to need to find the right activities to tire your canine without going outside much. Here are some alternatives to get rid of your Aussiedoodle's energy. Keep in mind that you'll still need considerable space.

1. Let your Aussiedoodle chase a laser pointer instead of you, since space is limited inside.

2. Tug of war is another great game that can help with other training as well. This is something you can start playing when your dog is a puppy, and it will also help him learn not to bite.

3. Hide and seek is a game you can play once your dog knows about proper behavior in the home. Since your Aussiedoodle will probably hear you wherever you hide, you can also make it a game of hide the toy. If you distract your pup while someone else hides the toy, your Aussiedoodle will have a good time trying to locate it.

4. Puzzle toys are a great way to get your dog to move around without you having to do much. Many of the games come with treats, and knowing Aussiedoodles, it won't be long before your dog figures out how to get the food out of the toy, so make sure you rotate various puzzles at playtime. Use these kinds of toys sparingly to avoid piling on the extra calories.

5. Poodles are popular circus performers for a reason, and that is something that you can really make use of if you love to train your dog. From obstacle courses to dancing, you can go online and look up unique dog tricks to see all of the possibilities. The training sessions can be a lot of fun, and they will stimulate your dog mentally as well as physically. It will also be a great way to entertain guests since your dog will likely want to play with everyone who comes through the door.

Photo Courtesy of
Allie Johnson

CHAPTER 14
Grooming – Productive Bonding

"Most Aussiedoodles won't shed their coat at all. That's not to be confused with losing strands of hair here and there. Everything that has hair loses some of it in the natural cycle. Sometimes an Aussiedoodle can lean too much toward the Aussie and shed lightly, but none of them will be as heavy as a purebred Aussie. If you are concerned about it, choose a puppy that has a curlier coat."

Adrian Booher
Sunset Hill Farm

The amount of effort required to keep your Aussiedoodle clean and looking good is going to depend on which one of the parents the dog takes after, particular their coat. Both breeds have some similar aspects in terms of grooming needs, but they also have their own weaknesses.

You'll need to regularly groom your Aussiedoodle's:

- Coat (bath and brushing)
- Eyes and ears
- Nails
- Teeth

Photo Courtesy of
Ashley Schow
Cottonwood Creek Doodles

Grooming Tools

"Best to remember that with a longer coated dogs that brushes just do not work. You need to get a very good comb and a slicker. Back combing weekly is the best course of care and be sure to pay special attention to behind ears, under legs and around the rear."

Joyce Wallace
Pecan Place Aussiedoodles

Aussiedoodles that have coats more like Australian Shepherds are easier to groom. A wavy coat will require a lot less work than a typical Poodle curl because curlier fur mats easier and can actually curl dirt into it, while wavy fur doesn't tend to trap nearly as much dirt.

You don't need too many tools to properly groom your Aussiedoodle. Make sure you have the following on hand before your puppy or adult dog arrives:

- A slicker or pin brush (Bark Space provides some details on the different types of brushes)

- Grooming comb (this one is optional, but can help curlier fur look fluffier)

- Detangling spray can be great to keep fur from tangling if your dog's coat is more Poodle-like

- Shampoo (check Bark Space for the latest recommendations)

- Nail trimmers

- Toothbrush and toothpaste (check the American Kennel Club for the latest recommendations)

FUN FACT
Coat Types and Colors

Since Aussiedoodles are a mix of two breeds with different coat types, you never know what coat type or color puppies will have. Aussiedoodles may have the tight curls of a Poodle, the shedding coat of an Australian Shepherd, or a wavy coat that's prone to tangling. Common colors include (but aren't limited to) blue merle, red merle, black, black and white, and tricolor.

Photo Courtesy of Nikki Stewart

Things To Know About Coat Management

Designer breeds are notoriously difficult to plan for in terms of coat management, especially if their coats are as varied as the Aussiedoodle (or any of the Doodle mixes since few breeds have coats similar to the Poodle). At the least, you will need to brush your adult Aussiedoodle twice a week. If your dog's coat is more like a Poodle's, plan to brush your dog three or four times a week. Beyond that, if you want to have the fur styled like the Poodle parent's coat, you can. If you prefer a more mellow approach, so long as you maintain the brushing routine, that's fine too. Because Aussiedoodles are considered hypoallergenic dogs, you aren't going to spend too much time cleaning up fur around the home.

Puppy

Brushing any puppy is usually an interesting challenge because the little guy is probably going to be incredibly wiggly and excited. Brushing will seem like playtime to him, and there is a good chance he will nip and try to knock the brush out of your hands. The No Nipping rule will apply here too, so make sure you keep it in mind and enforce it. Grooming a puppy requires patience and gentle coaxing. The wiggling and playing can be cute at first, but you still want to get him to stop that behavior so that you can complete the task – it will be much less cute when he is older and still thinks that brushing is playtime instead of cleaning time. As your puppy learns the routine, brushing will get easier. To help, brush your puppy after a tiring walk.

Cleaning The Eyes And Ears

When you bathe your Aussiedoodle, you need to be careful not to get water in his ears. You should also make a habit of regularly checking not only his coat for sores or rashes but also his eyes and ears. He may have allergies that will make the inside of his ears look red. A warm, moist pad can be used on the surface part of the ear. If redness doesn't look better in a day, make an appointment to visit the vet. If you see wax buildup, you can very gently wipe it away. Never put anything in your dog's ears though.

Cataracts are a fairly common problem for all dogs as they age. If you see cloudy eyes, have your Aussiedoodle checked. If he's developing cataracts, you may need to take the pup in to have them removed as cataracts can lead to blindness.

Photo Courtesy of
Brey Sanchez
Marley's Doodles

Bath Time

"Your Doodle isn't likely to smell bad, but my! A Doodle can get dirty! Bathing helps--and do-it-yourself dog wash facilities are increasingly easy to find and helpful."

Sheron MW Steele, PhD
XANADU of the Rockies

Given Aussiedoodles' size and short, dark coats, a bath every few months should be more than enough to keep your pup clean, especially if you're brushing him daily. Set your bath schedule for about once a quarter (four times a year), and your dog should be happy. Of course, if your Aussiedoodle gets dirty (which may happen whenever you go out exploring or hiking), then you'll need to take the time to bathe your canine.

Putting a dog this big into the bath really isn't recommended. Look for a place where you can wash your dog nearby or in the yard. Of course, during the cold months, you can probably skip the baths entirely since you likely won't be out as much.

After bathing, take the time to groom your Aussiedoodle just like you would after a bath. This will keep the tangles down.

"Do not bath them too often, or you risk stripping all the natural oil out of their skin."

Kristine Robards
Double R Doodles

Trimming The Nails

Cutting Aussiedoodles' nails is difficult because the nails are black like the dog's coat, which means that you may cut too much off and cause the quick to bleed. It's best to have an expert cut your dog's nails until you can see how it's done. If you do cut your Aussiedoodle's nails yourself, have some styptic powder near you in case you cut too much off.

To know when your pup needs those nails cut, pay attention to the sounds your dog makes when walking on harder surfaces to make sure the nails aren't clicking. If they are, then you should increase how often you get his nails trimmed.

Brushing The Teeth

Aussiedoodles need their teeth brushed often to avoid dental problems, and you probably will want to learn to do it yourself over having to visit a shop once a week. It's also nice to know how to do it if his breath smells bad or he ate something that smells foul.

You need to get a tooth-paste that is made for dogs. Hu-

HELPFUL TIP
Turn Brushing Time into Bonding Time

Aussiedoodle hair is prone to matting and requires daily brushing, especially if you want to keep any length on it. Train your puppy early to enjoy brushing and turn it into a daily bonding routine. Neither of you will be happy if brushing turns into a battle.

Photo Courtesy of Ariel Childers

man toothpaste can be toxic. The flavor of dog toothpaste will also make it easier to brush their teeth – or at least entertaining as they try to eat it. To start brushing your pup's teeth:

1. Put a little toothpaste on your finger and hold it out to your dog.

2. Let your dog lick the toothpaste.

3. Praise your dog for trying something new.

4. Put a little toothpaste on your finger, lift up your dog's upper lip, and begin to rub in circles along your Aussiedoodle's gums. Your pup will very likely make it difficult by constantly trying to lick your finger. Give your puppy praise when he doesn't wiggle too much.

   a. Try to move in a circular motion. This will be very tricky, especially with those sharp baby teeth.

   b. Try to keep the puppy still without putting the little pooch in a vise. As your puppy gets bigger, you'll need for him to sit for the cleaning voluntarily.

   c. Try to massage both the top and bottom gums. It is likely that the first few times you won't be able to do much more than get your finger in your dog's mouth, and that's okay. Over time, your puppy will learn to listen as training elsewhere helps your dog understand when you are giving commands.

5. Stay positive. No, you probably won't be able to clean the puppy's teeth properly for a while, and that is perfectly fine so long as you keep working at it patiently and consistently.

Once your dog seems all right with you brushing with your finger, try the same steps with a toothbrush. It may be a similar song and dance in the beginning, but it shouldn't take nearly so long. It could take a couple of weeks before you can graduate to a toothbrush, but even if it does take that long, it is still great bonding time.

CHAPTER 15
Health Issues – Parasites

"Aussiedoodles are sensitive to any medications with Ivermectin in them. Please watch what kind of flea/tick medications you use. No Ivermectin."

Mary Ann McGregor
Hearthside Country

Environmental factors largely determine whether or not your dog gets parasites. For example, if you live near woods, your dog is at a greater risk of ticks than a dog that lives in the city. Talk to your vet about particular environmental risks to your dog.

The Role Of Your Veterinarian

From getting annual vaccines updated to health checkups, regularly scheduled vet visits will make sure that your Aussiedoodle stays healthy. Since Aussiedoodles are such eager companions, it will be obvious when they aren't acting in the way that they normally do. You will notice the changes, especially if your Aussiedoodle stops following you around the house. Annual visits to the vet will ensure there isn't a problem that is slowly draining the energy or health from your dog.

Health checkups also make sure that your Aussiedoodle is aging well. If there are any early symptoms of something potentially wrong with your dog over the years (such as arthritis), you will be able to start making adjustments early in the process. The vet can help you come up with ways to manage pain and problems that come with the aging process and will be able to recommend adjustments to the schedule to accommodate your canine's aging body and diminishing abilities. This will ensure that you can keep having fun together without hurting your dog.

Vets will begin your pet on treatments for the different parasites and microscopic threats that your dog may encounter when he is outside, during interactions with other dogs, or from exposure to animals outside your home.

Photo Courtesy of Hunter Seidl

Fleas And Ticks

Given how much Aussiedoodles love to be out in the outdoors, they're at a much greater risk of both ticks and fleas than many other dogs, and neither parasite is easy to see because an Aussiedoodle has a dark coat. Therefore, you can't allow any lapse in treatment, even in the winter.

Make it a habit to check for ticks after every outing into the woods, or near long grass or wild plants. Comb through the fur and check the skin for irritation and parasites. Since you will be doing this often, you should be able to tell when a bump is a problem. Since your dog will be very happy to spend time with you, it shouldn't take as long as you might think –

HELPFUL TIP
Health Issues

Aussiedoodles may inherit congenital health issues from one or both parents. Some health issues they may be susceptible to include:

- Hip dysplasia, which can cause pain and lameness in the hips and back legs
- Progressive Retinal Atrophy (PRA), which can lead to blindness
- Detached retinas, which can cause blindness
- Cataracts, which can reduce vision
- Glaucoma, which can lead to blindness
- Epilepsy (seizures)
- Multiple Drug Sensitivity (MDS), a sensitivity to many types of drugs
- Hypothyroidism, which is when the thyroid gland doesn't release enough thyroid hormone
- Luxating patella (floating kneecap)
- Bloat, a life-threatening condition where the stomach twists
- Cancer
- Pancreatitis

it isn't as though you'll have to spend a lot of time struggling to get your Aussiedoodle to sit still for a tick check.

Fleas will be more problematic because they're far more mobile. The best way to look for fleas is to make it a regular part of your brushing sessions. You can also look for behavioral indicators, such as incessant scratching and licking. You will need to use flea preventative products on a regular basis once your puppy reaches an appropriate age.

The FDA has issued a warning about some store-bought treatments. Whether you look into purchasing treatments that have to be applied monthly or a collar for constant protection, you need to check the treatment to see if the ingredients include isooxazoline (included in Bravecto, Nexgard, Credelio, and Simparica) because this ingredient can have an adverse effect on pets. While other ingredients are safe for pets when used in the proper doses, if you use a product that is meant for a larger dog, it can be toxic to your dog. Consult with your vet about recommended treatments to ensure that you get the right dose of flea and tick repellant for your dog's size and needs. When you do start applying the treatment, monitor your dog for the following issues:

- Diarrhea/Vomiting
- Trembling
- Lethargy
- Seizures

Take your dog to the vet if you notice these issues.

Never use any product designed for a dog on a cat or vice versa. If your dog is sick, pregnant, or nursing, you may need to look for an alternative treatment. Flea collars are generally not recommended because they are known to cause problems in pets and people. If you have a cat or young children, you should choose one of the other options for keeping fleas and ticks off of your dog.

If you decide to purchase a flea treatment, make sure to read the packaging to find out when it is the right time to begin treating your dog based on the current age and size. Different brands have different recommendations, and you don't want to start treating your puppy too early. There are also very important steps to apply the treatment. Make sure you understand all of the steps before you purchase the flea treatment.

If you want to use natural products instead of chemical ones, set aside a few hours to research the alternatives and find out what works best for your Aussiedoodle. Verify that any natural products work before you buy them and make sure you consult with your vet. Establishing a regular schedule and adding it to the calendar will help you remember to treat your dog each month.

Aussiedoodles with allergies may develop hot spots that you think are fleas initially. Hot spots are inflamed areas of the skin that when left untreated can result in fur loss or a lot of itching. If you notice your dog scratching and can't find evidence of fleas, it could actually be an allergic reaction. Take your Aussiedoodle to the vet if you notice a lot of scratching but aren't sure of the reason.

Worms

Although worms are a less common problem than fleas and ticks, they can be far more dangerous. Your dog can actually become sick from worms that are carried by fleas and ticks. There are a number of types of worms that you should be aware of:

- Heartworms
- Tapeworms
- Hookworms
- Whipworms
- Roundworms

Unfortunately, there isn't an easy to recognize set of symptoms to help identify when your dog has worms. However, you can keep an eye out for these symptoms, and if your dog shows them, schedule a visit to the vet.

- Your Aussiedoodle is unexpectedly lethargic for at least a few days.
- Patches of fur begin to fall out (this will be noticeable if you brush your Aussiedoodle regularly) or if you notice patchy spaces in your dog's coat.

- If your dog's stomach becomes distended (expands) and looks like a potbelly.

- Your Aussiedoodle begins coughing, vomiting, has diarrhea, or has a loss in appetite.

If you aren't sure about any symptom, it's always best to get to the vet as soon as possible to check.

Heartworms

Heartworms are a significant threat to your dog's health and can be deadly as they slow and stop blood flow. You should be actively treating your dog for heartworms to ensure that this parasite does not have a home in your dog.

Fortunately, heartworms are among the easiest potential health problem you can prevent. There are medications that can ensure your Aussiedoodle does not get or have heartworms. To prevent this very serious problem, you can give your dog a chewable medication, topical medicine, or you can request shots.

This particular parasite is carried by mosquitoes, which are nearly impossible to avoid in most regions of the country. Since heartworms are potentially deadly, taking preventative measures is essential.

If a dog has heartworms, it will be costly and time-consuming to treat and cure, but if you adopt an adult Aussiedoodle, it will be well worth all of the work because of how amazing a dog they are.

1. The vet will first draw blood to conduct tests, which can cost as much as $1,000.

2. Treatment will begin with some initial medication, including antibiotics and inflammatory drugs.

3. Following a month of the initial medication, your vet will give your dog three shots over two months.

From the time when the vet confirms that your dog has heartworms until he or she says your dog is clear of the parasite, you have to keep your dog calm. Your vet will tell you how best to exercise your canine during this time. Considering your Aussiedoodle is likely to be energetic, this is going to be a very rough time for both you and your dog. You will need to be careful when your dog exercises because the worms are in your dog's heart, inhibiting blood flow. Getting your dog's blood pumping too much can kill him.

Treatment will continue after the shots are complete. After about six months, your vet will conduct another blood test to ensure that the worms are gone.

Once your dog is cleared of the parasites, you will need to be vigilant about medicating your dog against heartworms. You want to make sure that your poor little guy doesn't suffer through that again. There will be lasting damage to your dog's heart, so you will need to ensure that your dog does not over exercise. You also need to protect him from getting heartworms again in the future.

Intestinal Worms: Hookworms, Roundworms, Tapeworms, And Whipworms

These four parasites become a problem when your dog ingests them. All four of these worms thrive in your dog's intestinal tract, and they get there when your dog eats something contaminated with them. The following are the most common ways that dogs ingest worms:

- Feces
- Small hosts, such as fleas, cockroaches, earthworks, and rodents
- Soil, including licking it from their fur and paws
- Contaminated water
- Milk (if the mother has worms, she can pass it to young puppies when they eat)

The following are the most common symptoms and problems caused by intestinal parasites:

- Anemia
- Blood loss
- Coughing
- Dehydration
- Diarrhea
- Large intestine inflammation
- Weight loss

Hookworms can actually get into dogs (and humans) through the skin. If a dog rests in soil with hookworm larvae, the parasite can burrow through their skin. Vets will conduct a diagnostic test to determine if your dog has this parasite. If your dog does have hookworms, your vet will prescribe a de-wormer. You should visit a doctor because you can get hookworms, too.

Roundworms are kind of like fleas in that they are very common, and at some point in their lives, most dogs have to be treated for them. They primarily eat the digested food in your dog's stomach, getting the nutrients

Photo Courtesy of
Courtney Bentley

that your dog needs. It is possible for larvae to remain in your dog even after all of the adult worms have been eradicated. Mothers can pass these larvae to their puppies. This means if you have a pregnant Aussiedoodle, you will need to have her puppies periodically checked to make sure the inactive larvae aren't passed on to the puppies. If they are, the larvae will be activated. The mother will also need to go through the same testing to make sure they don't make her sick. In addition to the symptoms listed above, your Aussiedoodle may also appear to have a potbelly. You may also see them in your dog's excrement or vomit.

Tapeworms are usually eaten when they are eggs, usually carried by fleas or from the feces of other animals that have tapeworms. They develop in the canine's small intestine until they are adults. Over time, parts of the tapeworm will break off and be obvious in your dog's waste, which needs to be picked up to keep other animals from getting tapeworms. While they typically aren't fatal, they can cause weight loss while giving your dog a pot belly (depending on how big the worms get on your dog's intestines). Your vet can test your dog to see if he has tapeworms, and will prescribe a medication that you can give your dog, including chewables, tablets, or a medication you can sprinkle on your dog's food. There is a low risk of humans getting tapeworms, with kids being at the greatest risk because of the likelihood that they will play in areas where dogs have gone to the bathroom and not wash their hands and bodies enough afterward. It is possible to contract tapeworms if a person swallows a flea, which is possible if your dog and home have a serious infestation.

Whipworms grow in the large intestine, and in larger numbers, they can be fatal. Their name is indicative of their appearance, with their tails appearing thinner than the upper section. Like the other worms, you will need to have your dog tested to determine if he is sick.

Keeping up with flea treatments, making sure people pick up behind their pets, and watching to make sure your Aussiedoodle doesn't eat trash or animal waste are the best preventative measures to keep your dog safe from these parasites.

If your dog has hookworms or roundworms, these can be spread to you from your dog through skin contact. Being treated at the same time as your Aussiedoodle can help stop the vicious cycle of continually switching which of you has worms.

Preventative measures against all of these worms can be included with the preventative medication for heartworms. Talk to your vet about the different options to keep your pet from suffering any of these health problems.

Holistic Alternatives

Wanting to keep a dog from a lot of exposure to chemical treatments makes sense, and there are many good reasons why people are moving to more holistic methods. However, doing this does require a lot more research and monitoring to ensure that the methods are working – and more importantly, do not harm your dog. Unverified holistic medicines can be a waste of money, or, worse, they can even be harmful to your pet.

If you decide to go with holistic medication, talk with your vet about your options. You can also seek out Aussiedoodle experts to see what they recommend before you start using any methods you are interested in trying. Read what scientists have said about the medicine you are considering. There is a chance that the products you buy from a store are actually better than some holistic medications.

Make sure you are thorough in your research and that you don't take any unnecessary risks with the health of your Aussiedoodle.

Vaccinating Your Aussiedoodle

Photo Courtesy of Bri Kinnison

Vaccination schedules are almost universal for all dog breeds, including Aussiedoodles. The following list can help you ensure your Aussiedoodle receives the necessary shots on schedule. Make sure to add this to your calendar. As a reminder, no shots should be administered during the first vet visit. Your new dog already has enough stress with all of the changes in his life without adding illness. If your puppy is due for more shots soon after arriving at your home, that trip should be scheduled separately, once your puppy feels more comfortable in your home.

The following table provides details on which shots should be administered and when.

Timeline	Shot		
6 to 8 weeks	Bordetella	Leptospira	DHPP – First shot
	Lyme	Influenza Virus-H3N8	Influenza Virus-H3N2
10 to 12 weeks	Leptospira	DHPP – Second shot	Rabies
	Lyme	Influenza Virus-H3N8	Influenza Virus-H3N2
14 to 16 weeks	DHPP – Third shot		
Annually	Leptospira	Bordetella	Rabies
	Lyme	Influenza Virus-H3N8	Influenza Virus-H3N2
Every Three Years	DHPP Booster	Rabies (if opted for longer duration vaccination)	

These shots protect your dog against a range of ailments. Keep in mind that you will need to make shots an annual part of your dog's vet visits so that you can keep your pup safe. If you would like to learn more about the diseases these vaccinations protect your dog from contracting, check out the Canine Journal. They provide details about the ailments and other information that can help you understand why it is so important to keep up with the shots.

Environmental Allergies

Like people, dogs can have allergies, though it can be difficult to tell when a dog is having an allergic reaction. The scientific name for environmental allergies is atopic dermatitis, but it is more difficult to tell whether the problem is with the environment or the food you are giving your dog. The symptoms tend to be similar in dogs for both types of allergies:

- Itching/scratching, particularly around the face
- Hot spots
- Ear infections
- Skin infections
- Runny eyes and nose (not common)

Dogs often develop allergies when they are between 1 and 5 years old. Once they develop allergies, canines don't outgrow this problem. Usually

Photo Courtesy of Jenny Pettit

dog allergies are through skin exposure, but some can be allergic through inhaling microscopic particles (the common method for humans who are suffering allergies). Dogs can be allergic to the same things that humans are allergic to, such as dust, molds, and pollens.

Since the symptoms are the same for food and environmental allergies, you will need to talk to your vet about determining the cause. If your dog has a food allergy, all you have to do is change the food that you give your dog. If your dog has an environmental allergy, he will need medication, just as humans do. Because of this, you will want to know if the problem is from something seasonal (like pollen) or something year-round so you will know when to treat your dog.

Like with humans, completely eliminating the problem really isn't reasonable – there is only so much you can do to change the environment around your dog. There are several types of medications that can help your dog be less sensitive to the allergens.

- Antibacterial/Antifungal – There are several medications for these allergies, including shampoos, pills, and creams. These usually do not treat the allergy, but the problems that come with allergies, such as bacterial and yeast infections.

- Anti-inflammatory – An oral medication that is comparable to allergy medicine for people. You will need to be careful if you use these medications, monitoring your dog to see if there are any adverse effects. If your dog has a bad reaction, such as lethargy, diarrhea, or dehydration you should consult with your vet.

- Immunotherapy – A series of shots can help reduce your dog's sensitivity to whatever he is allergic to. This is something you can do at home, so you won't need to take your dog to the vet to complete the series. Scientists have been developing an oral version of the medication to make it easier to take care of your dog.

- Topical – This medication tends to be a type of shampoo and conditioner that will remove any sources for the allergies from your dog's fur. Giving your dog a warm (not hot) bath can also help relieve itching.

Talk with your vet about the medications that are available for your dog to determine the best treatment for your situation and your Aussie-doodle's needs.

CHAPTER 16
Genetic Health Concerns

"If the parents of your Aussiedoodle puppy are healthy - your Aussiedoodle should not have any health issues. However, you can have a DNA test done - checking for the MDR1 - multi drug resistance."

Mary Ann McGregor
Hearthside Country

As with all designer breeds, it is impossible to know exactly what health issues your canine will have. Trying to guess as to what ailments a dog is likely to inherit is tricky at best. Therefore, the best way to keep your canine healthy is to look for the ailments that are common to both of the original breeds. Since both of the parent breeds are well established, they are by now well known for having several genetic maladies that you will need to watch for in your pup. This is why regular vet visits are critical – you want to catch problems as early as possible.

All of the details on the genetic and common ailments of Aussiedoodles are found in Chapter 3. Making sure that the parents are healthy increases the likelihood that your puppy will remain healthy. However, there is still a chance that your dog will have one of these documented problems even if the parents don't, so you will still need to keep an eye on your friend.

CAUTION
Separation Anxiety

As a breed, Aussiedoodle are very prone to separation anxiety. If they had their way, they would be by your side 24/7. If possible, don't leave your puppy alone for long periods. Gradually leave him alone longer as he gets older. You can leave behind food puzzles and chew toys to keep your dog busy while you're gone, too.

Common Australian Shepherd Health Issues

As a working, medium-sized dog, Australian Shepherds have a number of ailments that you should monitor for as your dog ages.

Hip And Elbow Dysplasia

Hip and elbow dysplasia are common ailments for medium and larger sized dogs. Their diet (Chapter 12) as a puppy can help minimize the problem when they are adults. Both types of dysplasia are a result of the dog's hip and leg sockets being malformed that often leads to arthritis as the improper fit damages cartilage. The condition is possible to detect by the time a dog becomes an adult (around 2 years old for the Aussiedoodle). The only way to detect it though is through X-rays.

This is a problem that your Aussiedoodle may try to hide because he won't want to slow down. Your adult dog will walk a little more stiffly, or may pant even when it's not hot. It usually becomes more obvious as a dog nears his golden years, similar to how older people tend to change their gait to accommodate pain, your dog may do the same. Getting up may be a little more difficult in the beginning, and will likely get worse as he ages.

While surgery is an option in severe cases, most dogs can benefit from less invasive treatment:

- Anti-inflammatory medications – talk to your vet (dogs should not have large doses of anti-inflammatory drugs on a daily basis the way people do since aspirin and anti-inflammatories can damage your dog's kidneys)
- Lower the amount of high impact exercise your dog gets, especially on wood floors, tile, concrete, or other hard surfaces (given how much your dog probably loves to swim, you can move more to a swimming exercising regiment to keep them active without the jarring motions of walking and jogging on hard surfaces)
- Joint fluid modifiers
- Physical therapy
- Weight loss (for dogs who are overweight or obese)

Collie Eye Anomaly (Cea) And Colobomas

The disease can be mild, with little effect on your dog, but it can also cause blindness. The problem is caused by the dog's eye or eyes not properly forming. In the most severe cases, it can cause holes to develop in layers of the eye, resulting in complete vision loss and retinal detachment.

Photo Courtesy of
Ada Chan

You can have your dog tested to determine if it is a problem, and if so, it is treatable in most cases. There is no set of symptoms for this ailment as each dog that has it can have a different reaction to compensating for the changes in their vision. That is why testing is essential – you may not have any warning that there is something wrong with your dog. Vets can detect the problem as early as 5 to 8 weeks after the puppy is born. If your vet does find the problem in your dog, there really isn't a treatment or cure for the problem. Fortunately, most dogs are minimally affected by CEA. If your dog starts to show signs that his vision is affected, you will need to make adjustments to accommodate your dog's disability.

Another eye illness to watch for from the Australia Shepherd side is Colobomas, which keeps the dog's eye from fully developing. This problem can cause discomfort for your dog in bright light as your dog's iris is not properly formed, and may have holes in it.

If your dog squints or blinks a lot when you step out in the sun, it could be a sign that your dog has Colobomas. It is one of the problems that puppies should be tested for so that you can plan to properly take care of your dog if he has the issue. While light sensitivity tends to be the worst problem with Colobomas, it is associated with other eyes issues, like cataracts. There is no cure for Coloboma, but other issues associated with it can be treated. If your Aussiedoodle does have this ailment, try to accommodate for it by avoiding going outside when the sun is really bright, or stick to shady areas when you are outside.

Multiple Drug Sensitivity (Mds)

One of the reasons you need to talk with your vet about all types of medications (even over the counter medications) is because Australian Shepherds tend to have MDS. This means they are hypersensitive to medications. Even treatments as common as heartworm medications can be built up in the dog's brain, which can be toxic to your dog.

Puppies should be tested for MDS. If it is determined that a puppy has MDS, you will always need to be cautious about what medication you give your dog.

Hyperthyroid And Hypothyroid

Australian Shepherds don't tend to have these problems as often as Poodles do, but they can still be susceptible to both of these conditions. Hypothyroidism is more common than hyperthyroidism, but they are both problems related to improper functioning of the dog's thyroid gland. Both conditions are a result of the thyroid producing an incorrect amount of

Photo Courtesy of Ruby Hunter

hormones, causing your dog's metabolism to be either too fast (hyperthyroidism) or too slow (hypothyroidism).

If you notice your dog gaining or losing weight without any changes to food intake and exercise, this is very likely the cause. It can also cause your dog to be either more hungry or less hungry. In more severe cases, it can cause vomiting and diarrhea. In some cases, your dog may grow more or less fur too.

Your vet will prescribe a medication to treat either problem. The medication usually supplements the hormones that the thyroid is not producing or is overproducing.

Common Poodle Health Issues

Most of the Poodle sizes have the same health issues, so it doesn't matter if the parent is a Miniature or Standard Poodle. Many of these problems are treatable with minimal health risks if caught and treated early.

Addison's Disease

This can be a major health problem as your dog's adrenal gland may not be producing enough of the hormones of aldosterone and cortisol. Aldosterone regulates your dog's electrolytes and water. Cortisol help your dog deal with stress. It can destroy your dog's immune system, cause tumors to form, and increases the risk of cancer.

The following are symptoms of Addison's disease:

- Dehydration
- Depression
- Diarrhea
- Excessive Thirst
- Lethargy
- Poor Appetite
- Weakness
- Weight Loss
- Vomiting

166

If you notice these symptoms, take your dog to the vet as soon as possible to have him diagnosed. If your vet determines that your dog has Addison's disease, oral medication is typically recommended. It is possible that your dog will need to be medicated for the rest of his life. Your vet will monitor your dog to determine if that is necessary. Your dog should be able to resume normal meals and exercise once they start feeling the effects of the medication.

Bloat/Gastric Dilatation And Volvulus (Gdv)

GDV, more commonly known as bloat, is a problem with dog breeds that have larger chests. Their stomach can fill with gases, causing the stomach to bloat. In the worst cases, the gas can cause the stomach to twist, cutting off the entrance and exit from the stomach. Nothing can enter or leave your dog's stomach once the stomach twists. While the bloat stage is not lethal, once the stomach twists, it can kill your dog.

This is not a genetic disease, but a physiological problem because of the structure of large dogs with deep chests. The smaller mid-section of these dogs is what makes their stomach prone to bloat and twisting.

Prevention is the best way of dealing with this problem. While you can have surgery done to keep the stomach from twisting, this may not be the best method of treatment for Aussiedoodles (see MDS). You can reduce the risk of this problem by taking the following measures.

- Feed your dog two or three times a day (not just one meal)
- Add wet dog food to kibble (if you feed your dog commercial dog food)
- Ensure the dry dog food is calcium-rich

Your Aussiedoodle is at lower risk than a Poodle, especially if your dog is on the smaller side or has more of an Australian Shepherd body type.

Progressive Retinal Atrophy (Pra)

Similar to Colobomas, PRA causes light sensitivity because of problems with the retina. Puppies should be tested, so if you adopt your puppy from a breeder, you should have a guarantee against this particular problem.

Dogs with this condition usually start presenting with night blindness, which can make your dog more nervous. If you look at your dog's eyes, they may also reflect light more as the eyes deteriorate. It does affect both eyes, so the problem should show in both.

There is no treatment for the problem. Like many of the eye problems of the Australian Shepherd, you will need to learn to accommodate your dog's failing sight over time.

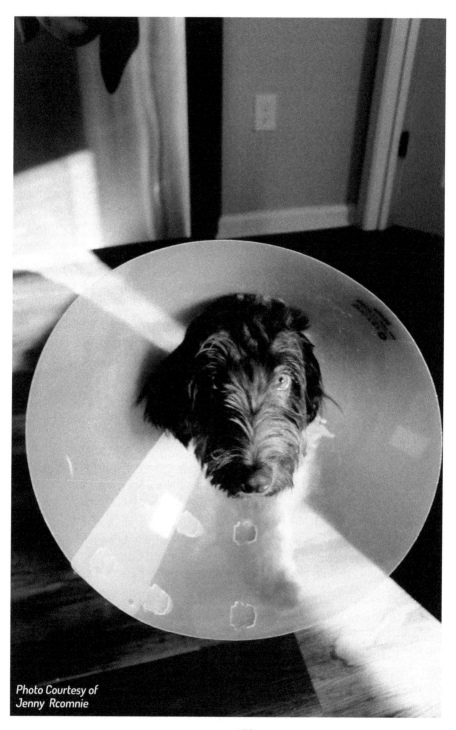

Photo Courtesy of
Jenny Rcomnie

Sebaceous Adenitis

This is a skin disease that destroys the sebaceous glands, which produce lubricating secretions. It can cause scales and hair loss. It is not life-threatening – it is a cosmetic problem. Your dog probably won't even notice the problem unless it has another kind of skin infection (which can be promoted by the disease).

It is a genetic disease, so your vet will need details on the parents. If that is not possible, your vet will run a few tests to determine if this is the problem.

If your pup has sebaceous adenitis, the vet will likely suggest a topical or oral therapy to help reduce the effects. More importantly, your dog may need an antibiotic as you likely won't notice the problem in the early days unless there is a secondary infection, which will require antibiotics to cure.

Luxating Patella

Luxating patella is a kneecap disease that is more common in Toy Poodles than in Standard Poodles. This ailment is genetic and your dog's kneecap may be dislocated.

If your dog has this problem, you may notice that he is skipping a step or limping on one leg. In more severe cases, your dog may not use the affected leg, meaning he is hopping around on three legs. When the kneecap slips back into place, your dog will resume a normal walk. As a dog ages, this problem will become worse as other issues present themselves, such as hip or elbow dysplasia or arthritis. Having multiple issues with the legs will make it harder for your dog to walk.

For the more severe cases, vets can perform surgery. Most dogs will not require surgery, but you do need to make sure that your dog does not overeat or become overweight as this will make walking that much harder.

Legg-Calve-Perthes Disease

Legg-Calve-Perthes disease is a degenerative bone disease that affects your dog's femurs. It is thought that it is caused by a disruption to the blood flow, which then weakens the bones. This can result in fractures and scarring to the surrounding tissues. One of the biggest concerns is that it typically leads to arthritis, which will make the problem a long-term concern.

If a dog has this problem, you will notice limping on the affected leg. Overtime, the limping will get worse. Touching the affected leg can be very painful for your dog, so you need to go to the vet if you suspect your dog has this condition.

It is a problem typically associated with smaller dogs, so it is less likely to be a problem if a Standard Poodle is one of the parents. If a Toy Poodle is a parent, your dog will be at greater risk.

Your vet may recommend pain medication. You will also be told to make sure your dog stays in a healthy weight range. Severe cases may require surgery.

Von Willebrand Disease

Potentially a major health problem for Miniature and Standard Poodles, Von Willebrand disease affects blood platelets by reducing how much protein they get. While Poodles are not at a high risk of the illness, it is very serious and there are no obvious symptoms associated with it. If your dog receives a cut and seems to bleed too much for too long, that is usually one of the first signs you will notice to indicate that your dog has this disease.

Like MDS, dogs with Von Willebrand disease cannot have many typical types of medications as medication like anti-inflammatories and penicillin thin the blood, making the situation worse.

Testing is vital so that you can make sure your dog doesn't get cut. If your dog does start bleeding, you will need to get to the vet as quickly as possible to stop the bleeding. In the event that too much blood is lost, your dog may need a transfusion. Considering the restrictions on your dog, your vet will discuss the best treatment, though regular doses of any medication are not recommended.

Hip And Elbow Dysplasia

The larger a dog is, the more likely it is they will have one or both of these problems. The symptoms, diagnosis, and treatment are the same, regardless of breed.

Hyperthyroid And Hypothyroid

This problem is more common in Poodles than Australian Shepherds, but the symptoms and disease are the same.

Where You Can Go Wrong

In addition to genetic problems, there are things that you can do that could damage your dog's health related to diet and exercise levels. If you follow the recommendations in Chapter 15, your dog will remain healthy longer. In addition to these problems already listed, the following are some of the potential issues you should be aware of and watch for signs of:

- Entropion – the dog's eyelids roll inward, damaging the cornea.

- Ectropion – the dog's eyelids roll outward; typically a condition in puppies that may go away by adulthood.

- Juvenile Laryngeal Paralysis & Polyneuropathy – a genetic disease that affects a dog's nerves. Usually it starts with the voice box, and then starts to affect other areas.

- Wet eczema – common to most breeds with such thick coats, the skin can become irritated very quickly.

Prevention & Monitoring

Monitoring your Aussiedoodle's weight is important at least once a quarter or twice a year. With hip and elbow dysplasia being a real genetic problem, additional weight will only worsen things. Your vet will likely talk to you if your dog is overweight because this not only puts a strain on the dog's legs, joints, and muscles, but it can also have adverse effects on your dog's heart, blood flow, and respiratory system. Make sure to talk to your vet if you notice that your Aussiedoodle is having any trouble. Those regular vet visits can help you address issues that you may not think are that big a deal. Sometimes the symptoms you notice are a sign of a future problem.

Photo Courtesy of Katherine Hassell

CHAPTER 17
Your Aging Aussiedoodle

Aussiedoodles typically have a lifespan of 10 to 12 years, though that may change as the breed history becomes longer than just a couple of decades. You may start to notice your dog slowing down between ages 8 and 9. Since small dogs aren't considered seniors until 9 and large dogs are considered seniors at 7.5 years, you should be watching your dog by the time he is 8 years old.

A dog may remain healthy his whole life, but his body still won't be able to do the same activities at 8 or 9 years that he could do at 2. The changes you make as your dog ages will be based on your Aussiedoodle's specific needs. For larger dogs, the decline often seems to happen a lot faster, while smaller dogs may not show signs of aging until much later. The thing is that the signs are there, but we really don't want to see them. The first signs are usually your dog's walking becomes a little stiffer or he starts panting more heavily earlier in the walk. Start to tone back the jogs, or stop jogging and just go for more energetic walks.

Be more aware of how your aging Aussiedoodle is doing when you go out walking or playing around the home. Your schedule is going to need to change as your canine slows down. Be careful to ensure that your pup doesn't overexert himself as Aussiedoodles may be too focused on having fun to realize they're hurting and need to stop to rest.

HELPFUL TIP
Quality of Life

Aussiedoodles live an average of 10-12 years. As he approaches his senior years, it's up to you to gauge your dog's quality of life. Hip dysplasia or arthritis could cause constant pain, for example. Luckily, we have the option to humanely end our pets' suffering when they no longer seem to be enjoying life.

There is a reason these are called the golden years – you can really enjoy them with your dog. You don't have to worry as much about him tearing things up out of boredom or getting over excited on walks any more. You can enjoy lazy evenings and peaceful weekends with some less strenuous exercise to break up the day. It's easy to make the senior years incredibly enjoyable for your Aussiedoodle and yourself by making the necessary adjustments that allow your dog to keep being active without overexertion.

Senior Dog Care

In most cases, caring for an older dog is much simpler than taking care of a younger dog, and Aussiedoodles are no exception.

When it comes to items that your older Aussiedoodle will need to access regularly, you should:

- Set water bowls out in a couple of different places so that your dog can easily reach them as needed. If your Aussiedoodle shows signs of having trouble drinking or eating, place slightly raised water dishes around the home to make it easier for him.

- Cover hard floor surfaces (such as tiles, hardwood, and vinyl). Use non-slip carpets or rugs.

- Add cushions and softer bedding for your Aussiedoodle. This will both make the surface more comfortable and help him stay warmer. There are bed warmers for dogs if your Aussiedoodle displays achy joints or muscles often. Of course, you also need to make sure he isn't too warm, so this can be a fine balancing act.

- To improve his circulation, increase how often you brush your Aussiedoodle.

- Stay inside in extreme heat and cold. Your Aussiedoodle is hardy, but an old canine cannot handle extreme changes as well as it once did.

- Use stairs or ramps for your Aussiedoodle wherever possible so that the old pup doesn't have to try to jump.

- Avoid moving your furniture around, particularly if your Aussiedoodle shows signs of having trouble with his sight or has dementia. A familiar home is more comforting and less stressful as your pet ages. If your Aussiedoodle isn't able to see as clearly as he once did, keeping the home familiar will make it easier for your dog to move around without getting hurt.

- If you have stairs, consider setting up an area where your dog can stay without having to go up and down too often.

- Create a space where your Aussiedoodle can relax with fewer distractions and noises. Don't make your old friend feel isolated, but do give him a place to get away from everyone if he needs to be alone.

- Be prepared to let your dog out more often for restroom breaks.

Photo Courtesy of
Liz Ingersoll Sandburg

Nutrition

With less exercise, your dog doesn't need as many calories, which means you need to adjust your pup's diet. If you opt to feed your Aussiedoodle commercial dog food, make sure you change to a senior food. Senior food is designed for the changing dietary needs of older dogs, with lower calories and more nutrients that the older dog body needs.

If you make your Aussiedoodle's food, take the time to research how best to reduce calories without sacrificing taste and talk to your vet. Your canine is going to need less fat in his food, so you may need to find something healthier that still has a lot taste to supplement the types of foods you gave your Aussiedoodle as a puppy or active adult dog.

Exercise

Since Aussiedoodles are so gregarious, they are going to be just as happy with extra attention from you as they were with exercise when they were younger. If you make fewer demands, decrease the number of walks, or in any way change the routine, your Aussiedoodle will quickly adapt to the new program. You will need to make those changes based on your dog's ability, so it's up to you to adjust the schedule and keep your Aussiedoodle happily active. Shorter, more frequent walks should take care of your Aussiedoodle's exercise needs, as well as helping to break up your day a little more.

Your dog will enjoy napping as much as walking, especially if he gets to cuddle with you. Sleeping beside you while you watch television or as you yourself nap is pretty much all it takes to make your older Aussiedoodle content, but he still needs to exercise.

The way your Aussiedoodle slows down will probably be the hardest part of watching him age. You may notice that your Aussiedoodle spends more time sniffing during walks, which could be a sign that your dog is tiring. It could also be his way of acknowledging that long steady walks are a thing of the past and so he is stopping to enjoy the little things more. Stopping to smell things may now give him the excitement that he used to get by walking farther.

While you should be watching for your dog to tire, he may let you know. If he is walking slower, looking up at you, and flopping down, that could be his way of letting you know it's time to return home. If your canine can't manage long walks, make the walks shorter and more numerous and spend more time romping around your yard or home with your buddy.

Mental Stimulation

Just because your Aussiedoodle can't walk as far doesn't mean that his brain isn't just as focused and capable. As he slows down physically, focus more on activities that are mentally stimulating. As long as your Aussiedoodle has all of the basics down, you can teach him all kinds of low-impact tricks. At this point, training could be easier because your Aussiedoodle has learned to focus better and he'll be happy to have something he can still do with you.

New toys are another great way to help keep your dog's mind active. Be careful that the toys aren't too rough on your dog's older jaw and teeth. Tug of war may be a game of the past (you don't want to hurt old teeth), but other games such as hide and seek are still very much appreciated. Whether you hide toys or yourself, this can be a game that keeps your Aussiedoodle guessing. There are also food balls, puzzles, and other games that focus on cognitive abilities that your dog can really appreciate as he knows that he isn't as capable physically as he once was.

Some senior dogs do suffer from cognitive dysfunction (CCD) syndrome, a type of dementia. It is estimated that 85% of all cases of dementia in dogs go undiagnosed because of how difficult it is to pinpoint the problem. It manifests more as a problem of temperament.

If your dog begins to act differently, you should take him to the vet to see if he has CCD. While there really isn't any treatment for it, your vet can recommend things you can do to help your dog. Things like rearranging the rooms of your home are strongly discouraged as familiarity with his surroundings will help your dog feel more comfortable and will reduce stress as he loses his cognitive abilities. Fortunately, neither parent breed is prone to mental issues as they age. Mental stimulation will help to fight CCD, but you should plan to keep your dog mentally stimulated regardless of whether or not he exhibits symptoms of dementia.

Regular Vet Exams

Just as humans go to visit the doctor more often as they age, you'll need to take your dog to see your vet with greater frequency. The vet can make sure that your Aussiedoodle is staying active without overdoing it, and that there is no unnecessary stress on your older dog. If your canine has sustained an injury and hidden it from you, your vet is more likely to detect it.

Your vet can also make recommendations about activities and changes to your schedule based on your Aussiedoodle's physical abilities and any changes in personality. For example, if your Aussiedoodle is panting more now, it could be a sign of pain from stiffness. This could be difficult to distinguish given how much Aussiedoodles pant as a rule, but if you see other signs of pain, schedule a visit with the vet. Your vet can help you determine the best way to keep your Aussiedoodle happy and active during the later years.

Common Old-Age Ailments

Chapters 4 and 16 cover illnesses that are common or likely with an Aussiedoodle, but old age tends to bring a slew of ailments that aren't particular to any one breed. Here are the things you will need to watch for (as well as talking to your vet about them).

- Diabetes is probably the greatest concern for a breed that loves to eat as much as your Aussiedoodle does, even with 2 hours of daily exercise most of the dog's adult life. Although it is usually thought of as a genetic condition, any Aussiedoodle can become diabetic if not fed and exer-

Photo Courtesy of Candy Trosper

cised properly. This is another reason why it's so important to be careful with your Aussiedoodle's diet and exercise levels.

- Arthritis is probably the most common ailment in any dog breed, and the Aussiedoodle is no exception. If your dog is showing signs of stiffness and pain after normal activities, talk with your vet about safe ways to help minimize the pain and discomfort of this common joint ailment.

- Gum disease is a common issue in older dogs as well, and you should be just as vigilant about brushing his teeth when your dog gets older as you were at any other age. A regular check of your Aussiedoodle's teeth and gums can help ensure this does not become a problem.

- Loss of eyesight or blindness is relatively common in older dogs, just as it is in humans. Unlike humans, however, dogs don't do well with wearing glasses. Have your dog's vision checked at least once a year and more often if it is obvious that his eyesight is failing.

- Kidney disease is a common problem in older dogs, and one that you should monitor for the older your Aussiedoodle gets. If your canine is drinking more often and having accidents regularly, get your Aussiedoodle to the vet as soon as possible and have him checked for kidney disease.

Enjoying The Final Years

The last years of your Aussiedoodle's life can be just as enjoyable (if not more so) than the earlier stages since your dog has mellowed. All of those high energy activities will give way to cuddles and relaxing. Having your pup just enjoy your company can be incredibly nice (just remember to keep up his activity levels instead of getting too complacent with your Aussiedoodle's newfound love of resting and relaxing).

Steps And Ramps

Aussiedoodles may or may not be big, but even if your Aussiedoodle is on the smaller end, you shouldn't pick him up to carry him upstairs or put him in the car. Steps and ramps are the best way to safely ensure your Aussiedoodle can maintain some level of self-sufficiency as he ages. Also, using steps and ramps provides a bit of extra exercise.

What To Expect

Your Aussiedoodle probably isn't going to suffer from fear that you are less interested in spending time together; too much of the day will go to napping. He or she will continue to be a loving companion, interacting with you at every opportunity – that does not change with age. Your canine's limitations should dictate interactions and activities. If you are busy, make sure you schedule time with your Aussiedoodle to do things that are within those limitations. It is just as easy to make an older Aussiedoodle happy as it is with a young one, and it is easier on you since relaxing is more essential to your old friend.

Vet Visits

As your Aussiedoodle ages, you are going to notice the slow-down, and the pains in your Aussiedoodle's body are going to be obvious just like in an older person. You need to make sure that you have regular visits with your vet to make sure that you aren't doing anything that could potentially harm your Aussiedoodle. If your Aussiedoodle has a debilitating ailment or condition, you may want to discuss the options for ensuring a better quality of life, such as wheels if your Aussiedoodle's legs begin to have serious issues. In the worst cases, you may want to discuss the quality of your Aussiedoodle's life with the vet.

Preparing To Say Goodbye

This is something that all dog parents (well, pet parents really) don't want to think about, but as you watch your Aussiedoodle slow down, you will know that your time with your sweet pup is coming to an end. Given they don't have a long history, the rate of their decline could vary. Most working dogs tend to suddenly decline, making it very obvious when you need to start taking extra care of their aging bodies. They have trouble on smoother surfaces or can't walk nearly as far as they once did. It's certainly sad, but when it starts to happen, you know to begin to prepare to say goodbye.

Some dogs can continue to live for years after they begin to slow down, but most working dogs don't make it more than about a year or two. Sometimes dogs will lose their interest in eating, will have a stroke, or other problem that arises with little warning. Eventually, it will be time to say goodbye, whether at home or at the vet's. You need to be prepared, and that is exactly why you should be making the most of these last few years.

Talk to your family about how you will care for your dog over the last few years or months of his life. Many dogs will be perfectly happy, despite their limited abilities. Some may begin to have problem controlling their bowel movements, while others may have problems getting up from a prone position. There are solutions to all of these problems. It is key to remember that quality of life should be the primary consideration, and since your dog cannot tell you how he feels, you will have to take cues from your dog. If your dog still seems happy, there is no reason to euthanize him. At this stage, your dog is probably perfectly happy just sleeping near you for 18 hours a day. That is perfectly fine as long as he still gets excited about walking, eating, and being petted. The purpose of euthanasia is to reduce suffering, not to make things more convenient for yourself. This is what makes the decision so difficult, but your dog's behavior should be a fairly good indicator of how he is feeling. Here are some other things to watch to help you evaluate your dog's quality of life:

- Appetite
- Drinking
- Urinating and defecation
- Pain (noted by excessive panting)
- Stress levels

- Desire to be active or with family (if they want to be alone most of the time, that is usually a sign that they are trying to be alone for the end)

Talk to your vet if your dog has a serious illness to determine what the best path forward is. They can provide the best information on the quality of your dog's life and how long your dog is likely to live with the disease or ailment.

If your dog gets to the point when you know that he is no longer happy, he can't move around, or he has a fatal illness, it is probably time to say goodbye. This is a decision that should made as a family, always putting the dog's needs and quality of life first. If you decide it is time to say goodbye, determine who will be present at the end.

Once at the vet's office, if it is decided to euthanize the dog, you can make the last few minutes very happy by feeding your dog the things that he couldn't eat before. Things like chocolate and grapes can put a smile on his face for the remaining time.

You can also have your dog euthanized at home. If you decide to request a vet to come to your home, be prepared for additional charges for the home visit. You also need to determine where you want your dog to be, whether inside or outside, and in which room if you decide to do it inside.

Photo Courtesy of Gwendolyn Simon

Make sure at least one person is present so that your dog is not alone during the last few minutes of his life. You don't want your dog to die surrounded by strangers. The process is fairly peaceful, but your dog will probably be fairly stressed. He will pass within a few minutes of the injection. Continue to talk to him as his brain will continue to work even after his eyes close.

Once your dog is gone, you need to determine what to do with the body.

- Cremation is one of the most common ways of taking care of the body. You can get an urn or request a container to scatter your dog's ashes over his favorite places. Make sure you don't dump his ashes in places where that is not permitted. Private cremation is more expensive than communal cremation, but it means that the only ashes you get are from your dog. Communal creation occurs when several pets are cremated together.

- Burial is the easiest method if you have your pet euthanized at home, but you need to check your local regulations to ensure that you can bury your dog at home as some locations have made this practice illegal. You also need to consider the soil. If your yard is rocky or sandy, there are problems with trying to bury your pet at home. Also, don't bury your pet in your yard if it is near wells that people use as a drinking source, or if it is near wetlands or waterways. Your dog's body can contaminate the water as it decays. You can also look into a pet cemetery if there is one in your area.

CPSIA information can be obtained
at www.ICGtesting.com
Printed in the USA
LVHW080609020222
709980LV00002B/5